Stories of Truth and Triumph

Stories of Truth and Triumph

First published in September 2020

ISBN: 9798683675134
Editors: Lisa King, Nilam Dattani,
Designs: Jodie Lee Liggett

Contributors:
Astrid Phillips, Chantal Ul Haq-Weedon, Yasemin Akcakoca, Kath Wynne-Jones, Jodie Lee Liggett, Lara Costa, Leila Singh, Christina (Tina) Valentine, Talat (Anwer) Cheema-Ahmad, Nilam Dattani, Mir Kamran Ali, Janine Dunn, Aly Jones, Michelle Watson and Lisa King.

Contents

Artists Interpretation Of Her Design

Symbolism

Of images used

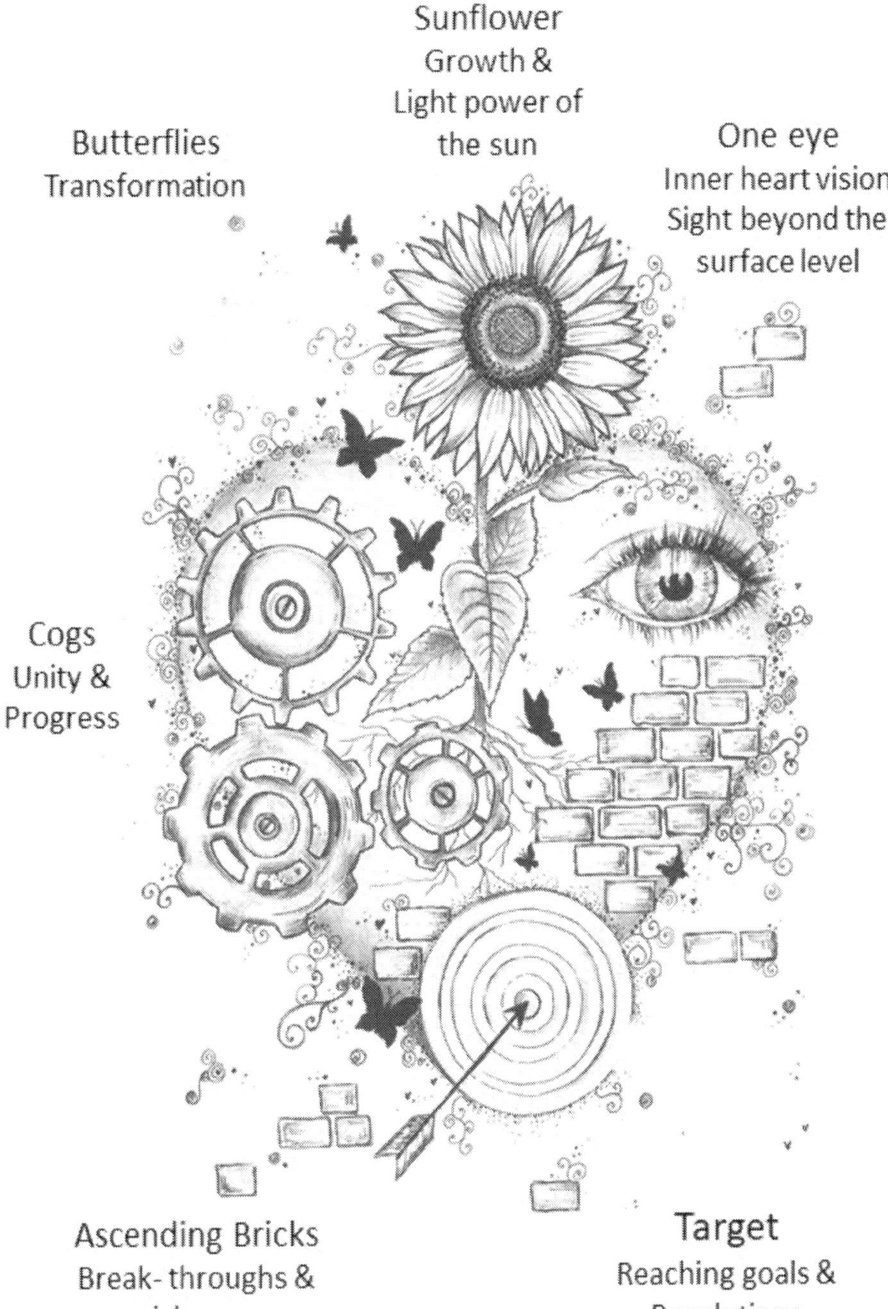

Foreword

On my journey through life, I have come to realise that one of the greatest powers that be is unity, especially the unity that breeds transformation and makes impact. This is exactly what I have seen working alongside the dedicated members and authors of the CFG (Clarity, Focus & Growth Collective) Family founded by a phenomenal woman and friend that I have come to know, appreciate and love – Lisa King . As you read this book you will not only be inspired and touched by the powerful stories these authors have shared, but the fact that they are using it to make a difference will indeed encourage you to not allow your past to prevent you from living your desired future.

The impact that we make on society depends upon how we overcome our most difficult moments. This book deals with the personal challenges each author has experienced and how they are now using their stories and expertise to change lives. This book will not only open your eyes to the many difficulties people face today but also you will receive tips on how to rise above your own challenges and turn your downsides of them into the upside of renewing your life. You are about to embark on a truly awe-inspiring journey and will realise that you are not on your own, someone else out there has walked a similar path that you are now on and have been able to use those dark moments to become a light for others.

In the pages that follow my foreword you will be taken back to some of those dark moments, but on finishing you will realise that there is indeed light at the end of the tunnel. To Lisa and all the authors that shared their stories in such a generous and touching way congratulations and thank you, for sharing your story. You are about to transform lives, there is no greater teacher than those

who have walked the walk and not allowed fear to keep them silent. The true light of the world are the ones that shine and not the ones that are hidden, because a light hidden cannot be seen by those who need it to walk their path.

Enjoy reading this amazing book, be inspired and shine your light x

Michelle Watson
Breakfree Forever Consultancy Ltd

Message from Lisa King
The Founder of Clarity, Focus and Growth Collective and the Stories of Truth and Triumph Book Series

We all have times when challenges are all consuming and it can feel like the road ahead is so daunting, and sometimes that road can feel too much and permanent choices can be made to end the pain. Especially now, at the time of publishing this book (2020), the world is dealing with huge changes, with mental health being impacted on a huge scale. So I believe this book will help you to see that you can create the change you want for yourself. In short, this is a book of HOPE.

Many years ago I endured my own defining experience, and at that time I needed to know there was hope, and finding the right people who could guide me and reassure me was a huge challenge. I knew there were many stories of truth and triumph that needed to be shared to inspire others. This is when my vision for this book and wider venture was born.

However, I was waiting for the right people to come together to make it happen, now the right people have come together, and are sharing their stories in a real, raw and vulnerable way.

Each of these authors have shared some or all of their stories to empower, inspire and guide you, and show you that you can get through it, you can push forward and reach the heights that you want to achieve in your life. Keep going, one step at a time.

One of my favourite quotes is by Chinese Philosopher Lao Tzu:
"The Journey of a Thousand Miles Starts with the First Step"

Many of us need assistance while we are taking these steps and the consequence of not doing so, we know can be fatal. In honour of a very special lady, in Becky's memory, and as a lasting legacy

to her, we have partnered with Megan's Space, a charity that has shared vision and goals. All profits from St*ories of Truth and Triumph* are being donated to Megan's Space. Megan's Mum, Jenny, shares her story and vision later in the book.

Anybody that has ever worked on a publishing project will know how challenging it is, and I absolutely could not have done this without the assistance of many people. There is always a risk to singling out individuals, and I thank everybody that has helped me. However, I want to say a huge thank you to Nilam & Jodie for welcoming my idea with amazing enthusiasm and energy. Your support and huge contribution has been immense and I am truly grateful. Thank you also to Michelle for your help and for the amazing support and help from all our authors, you are all truly amazing.

Lisa x

The Power Of My Best Friend Loneliness

Astrid Phillips

I wish I could say that she didn't know what the future held for her, but she did, and she knew it was not going to be very good! What do you do when your Best Friend asks you for help, but you are not quite sure how you can help except be there for them anytime they need you.

Let me take you back in time to November 2008.

We were in the doctor's waiting room in the Royal Marsden Hospital in Surrey. There was that clinical, sterile smell, white floors, white walls. The sunlight was streaming through the window and bouncing off the floor. It was a warm sunny day. To our left was a trolley bed and a white folding wheelie screen. In front of us we could see a brown wooden desk and the back of the computer monitor. We were waiting for some results.

My Best Friend was sitting next to me. She was a strong, powerful independent married Black Woman. She was always determined to reach any goal that she set herself, there was no stopping her and she was a force to be reckoned with. If you wanted to know the truth, then she was the person to ask, she would always speak the truth as she saw it. She was not backward in coming forward, in fact once met never forgotten.

I admired her and looked up to her. Always well-presented from head to toe. Only today this was not the person I saw! She appeared slouched in the chair like a child who had been told off and was sulking, gripping the sides of the chair. There is a click on

the door and the doctor walks in, in silence, and he takes a seat.

The doctor who is a George Clooney look a like but older with glasses, raises his head, he looked up but down his nose through his glasses and said 'Mrs. Phillips, you have Stage 3 Breast Cancer, which is advanced and the most aggressive! You will have to start treatment immediately if you want any chance of survival. If you had come to us earlier then maybe, we could have started your treatment earlier and the prognosis could have been different.

As I heard those words, my heart sank, I took a sharp intake of breath and tried to hold back the tears. I couldn't speak, I felt like I was choking, I couldn't get the words out. I lost my voice for what seemed like an age, however my sadness turned to hurt, my hurt then turned to frustration and rage all at the same time. My head was a tornado of emotions. Anger and rage was building inside of me, not at my Best Friend, but at the Doctor for what he had said. It was as if he had no feelings, no empathy just cold harsh words to a woman who was already devastated and suffering by the news she already knew, having been part of the medical profession. "What do you mean, if she had come to you earlier" I said quite indignantly. "Mrs Phillips should have come to us as soon as she found the lump in her breast, which was back at the beginning of September". Good thing I waited to hear what he said as back at the beginning of September was my birthday and we had planned dinner and a show. I couldn't be angry as I realised, my Best Friend had waited for me to have my birthday before she shared with me her news. Being a nurse and midwife, she knew the consequences of what she had!! "So Doctor, how soon can we book the appointment to get treatment?", "I will get the nurse to come in and explain everything to you", was his reply. "No" I said, trying desperately to keep my anger in check while staying strong for my Best Friend "You explain everything, you are

the doctor". He got up and said again "I will get the nurse" and before I could say anything else, he was gone.

My eyes started to fill up but I had to be strong, it was my turn to be the supportive one, I had to be strong for my Best Friend. She had always been there for me and now it was my turn, my turn to be strong, my turn to be there for her. How could I help, what could I do? This diagnosis meant that my Best Friend was going to leave me at some point in the future. How was I going to deal with that? How was I going to face losing my Best Friend? I suddenly heard her take a sharp intake of breath as if trying not to cry but I saw the tears rolling down her face. All I could do was reach out and hold her hand, I squeezed tight but then I had to hug her. I couldn't stop the flood of tears as I held her in my arms, I was scared of what was to come, fearful of the future as I felt deep down inside that this was going to be the beginning of the end.

Mrs. Phillips was my mum and my Best Friend. She was a proud woman and didn't want anyone to feel awkward or sorry for her, so we were instructed not to tell anyone. What little time and life she had left she wanted to make the most of it, spend her money on whatever she wanted, without having to worry, and live life on her terms. She was going to decide who, when and if people would be told about her Breast Cancer. She had already lost her nursing friend Alma, a number of years earlier and saw how other people had treated her and didn't want the same thing for herself. She continued to go to church every Sunday and went on to live for another 2 years.

On Sunday 15th August, she didn't have the energy to go to church so Pastor Johnson, knowing how poorly she was came to her to pray and say mass with her. On the Monday we had to call the doctor as mum was getting progressively worse and the dose of morphine that she was now being prescribed was not enough to

completely take away the pain. The local doctor came to visit as he knew the situation, the decision was made that it was time for her to go to the hospice. Mum had always wanted to be home with family and not in a hospice but she had had enough, that time had come. I remember mum hugging me and whispering in my ear 'I love you but it's time!

By Monday evening mum was at the hospice. I remember having to call my brother at work to explain where mum was and trust me it didn't take him long to get there! I made a few calls to let people know what was happening and where she was in the hospice.

Because no-one knew the extent of her sickness it was hard to explain in a convincing way how sick she really was. Mum was able to have her church family and immediate family around her. We sang and prayed with her, which I know was a blessing for her. However, in the early hours of 17th August 2010 mum lost her fight for life and passed away peacefully in the Macmillan Hospice in Clapham, with my brother by her side. Dad and I were dashing home to freshen up and come back but we were too late. Looking back on it now, I think that mum didn't want a fuss and because my brother was getting married on 25th September that same year, I truly believe that she waited for dad and I to go so she could spend her last moments with my brother. She wanted the focus of the wedding to be on him and her soon to be daughter in law and not on her because of her illness. She was no longer able to hide how poorly she was or how much pain she was in.

A loved ones death can make you quite lonely, especially when you find yourself on your own and there is no-one to share your time with. Well, that was now me! I went into practical mode, hiding my emotions, sorting out the funeral, getting the death certificates collected. I had decided that we would have the wake

wake at home and that Mum would be buried as soon as possible.

Isn't it surprising how people have an opinion on what you should or shouldn't do and how you should do it? The immediate family are the ones who decide what happens in line with the wishes of the deceased!! I was determined to ensure that all the arrangements were done as soon as possible so that it gave my brother and his wife to be, time before their wedding, which was now only 1 month away.

I sorted out the burial plot, the funeral directors, the location of her celebration of life. Mum's long-life Best Friend who had emigrated to Canada and her sister came over. Both of them came with me to the funeral parlour to dress mum's body, as I wanted to make sure that she looked her very best. She would be well dressed and that included her jewellery!! I think she would have come back and haunted me if I didn't! I had been shopping earlier in the morning and bought a pair of pink socks but ended up having to put them on my mum's feet as her shoes would not fit! The socks matched the outfit she was dressed in, it was the outfit she had bought with her future daughter in law, Seema, to wear to their wedding! Mum would have been so proud. She looked the part and her make-up made her look as though she was asleep.

Can you believe that on the day of the funeral, I managed to lock myself out of my flat!! My friend Sonia was collecting the funeral cards for the church, as the funeral was being held at the church that she went to, along with the hall that was next to the church for Mum's celebration of life. Imagine, the door has shut behind me and the keys and my mobile are in the flat, the spare keys are at my parents but I didn't have my car as it was in the garage! I went across the road to the hardware store and asked to borrow their ladders, so that I could climb into my kitchen window to get back into my flat and continue getting ready! Picture those wooden

ladders leaning at a 45° angle against the red brick wall, as you looked half way up the wall you can see the open window and that was where I was heading for. Whist the men from the hardware shop held the bottom of the ladder steady for me, I climbed up in my black heels, my black and white dress, my hair, nails and jewellery all co-ordinated, to get back into my flat, just before I was due to leave to go to my parents house for the funeral. It was a morning to remember.

When I got to my parents' house and told the story to everyone, they laughed and said it was mums last laugh and trying to get me to calm down. For the rest of the day, I was on autopilot and the only things I remember was how packed the church was for the funeral. There was standing room only and even then not everyone could fit into the church. I remember walking behind the coffin into the church with my future sister in law. I remember having my speech typed and in plastic sleeves so if I cried it would not blur the notes that I had. My final words to my mum being 'I am my Mother's Child' and everyone stood up and started clapping and smiling knowing how true that was. I was her mini-me!! At the graveside I took control of the shovel to cover the coffin, dressed immaculately and in my heels and the rest of my girly cousins all joining in with me before we then handed over to my brother Ian and his male cousins.

I know my mum would have loved the day, however, that night when I got home, I was all alone. For the first time I really felt the emptiness of being home alone. Loneliness was my new best friend, but not in a good way, I didn't want to do anything, go anywhere, I avoided people and conversations all the time. I felt that there was no-one to talk to who would understand, as no-one I knew had lost a parent. No-one to hug me & tell me everything was going to be alright.

Have you ever wished that you had more time? And if you had your time again, would you do things differently? Time goes by, no matter what you do to stop it. Once it has gone, you will never get it back, no matter who you are in this world, there is no substitute for time.

For the next 6 years, I call them my 'Wilderness Years' I withdrew into myself, only talking to people when I had to. I was on autopilot. I would go to work, put on a brave face, smile, do my work and as soon as my shift was over, I would get in my car and go home, I couldn't get out of work fast enough. Once I got in and closed the door, I was back with my best friend loneliness, and I felt safe, but I felt empty inside. My brother had his wife, and my dad had my mum's other best friend, who was married to his brother, as well as mum's sister, who he spoke to on the phone to Canada.

It was hard, loneliness was my new Best Friend but not in a good way. I was having my own pity party every day. How was this living life on my terms, how had I gone from being an ambitious, independent and courageous woman, who chose to maximise her earning potential and live abundantly. Leaving the corporate world as a Regional IT Project Manager to set up her own business, to ending up so unhappy, fearful and suffering with mild depression and having a silent breakdown.

I had kept everything to myself, I had convinced myself that that was how it was meant to be. I didn't want to ask for help, I didn't want their pity. The story I was telling myself was to live life quietly, don't burden anyone else as no one else would understand. No-one else would be able to help and I'm definitely not speaking to strangers. I didn't have my cheerleader, my mentor, my accountability partner, so what was the point? I no longer knew 'Why'. I had lost my mojo. I was suffering emotional and physical

stress, I could not concentrate on anything, I felt disconnected, I had lost my voice.

In May 2015, just after my mum's birthday I heard a song on the radio – "you are not alone, I am here with you, and though I am far away, I am here to stay, you are not alone, I am here with you, and though we're far apart I am always in your heart". It felt as though my mum was talking to me. The tears filled my eyes and I cried uncontrollably. I actually cried myself to sleep. I had not really cried, in all that time, not really.

When I woke up I actually felt better, like a weight had been lifted. I then heard the song by the Lighthouse Family "You could be lifted from the shadows, L-I-F-T-E-D". WOW, they were talking to me! . . I was being lifted from the shadows. It was as though I was having a transformation.

Before my mum passed away I was a Woman In Leadership, I was a Regional Manager leading teams in the Corporate World, but right now, I could not lead myself. I had to Level Up and get out of the 'funk' I was in, in order to be the person I knew I would be and wanted to be. At the very minimum, go back to being that inspired leader I knew I could be.

I had to admit to myself that I was not perfect, there is no such thing as perfect, just progress over perfection. I was not living, I was just existing and surviving. I took fear to mean Face Everything And Run instead of Face Everything And Rise. There was power in finding my voice, asking for help and I had forgotten that. As a child I didn't have problems asking for what I wanted. I didn't even have a problem with being alone, in fact I had 5 years on my own until my brother came along. I had moved out of my parents' house at age 23 to go live by myself, so it was nothing new. However, it was very different this time!

When I left the Corporate World, I was going to be a CEO of my own business and be my own boss. What happened to me? I needed to regain that drive and determination. Once upon a time I had courage, I was fearless, I would take on anything and anyone that got in the way of what I wanted to achieve. Where had that Woman gone? I wanted her back, I wanted that Warrior Goddess back. She had been like 'Sleeping Beauty' asleep for 6 years but that song had been the 'kiss' that woke her up.

No circumstance or person has the power to take away your courage and fearlessness unless you let that happen, which is exactly what I had done. I began to realise that I am not alone, I am not the only one who has lost someone special out of their life and experienced grief.

Here is where The **W.I.L.L** Women Academy was born. I had been a **W**oman **I**n **L**eadership and knew how to **L**evel Up to take the next step on that Corporate Ladder to get myself up to Regional Level. I had completed all the training to know how to start and run my own business and if I could Awaken the Warrior Goddess Within, I could do it again. I could do better, be better and have better than I had before.

If this story has resonated with you, I hope that I have given you the courage to take back your power and at the very least take the first step into your next chapter of life. You are not alone, you are courageous, you are powerful, strong and a beautiful woman. Don't wait for anyone else's approval, give yourself permission to be exactly who you want to be and live life on your terms.

Recognise that you can be, do or have anything that you put your mind to. Always strive to be confident as well as the best version of yourself. Ensure that you are using your time wisely and not letting it pass you by. Believe in You. Be happy healthy and enjoy

life. When you leave this world be the legacy you want to leave?

I hope that you will join me in The W.I.L.L Women Academy (Women in Leadership Level-Up) where you will be with other like-minded women who secretly know what they are capable of. Women who will support each other in this community. Women who want to Level-Up from where they are in their lives. Women who want to awaken and unleash that Warrior Goddess within to reclaim their time, maximise their earning potential and live life on their terms.

Author: Astrid Phillips

A quirky fact about me: As my brother would say "I jumped out of a perfectly good airplane" to get over my fear of falling & heights !! It was such an awesome experience, I went and did it another 5 times!!

What I do now: Astrid Phillips is an Award Winning Speaker, Coach & Mentor for Professional Business Women in Leadership who want to reclaim their time, maximise their earning potential & live life on their terms to have the freedom to improve their Health and Wealth for their family & loved ones. Astrid previously worked in Corporate for 20 years, working her way up the Corporate ladder to become a Regional IT Project Manager for the South of England, Jersey Guernsey, Isle of Man & Gibraltar. She was successfully running a business, so decided to leave on her terms and to it for herself!

Astrid, is the Founder & CEO of her business called W.I.L.L Women Academy (Women In Leadership Level-Up), that coaches women on the best way to step up into Senior Management levels, as well as Women who have had enough of their Corporate, Retail or Private Sector roles and are ready to leave to start their own business. She also coaches start-up Entrepreneurs.

Astrid is currently writing a book called Success Without the Sacrifice- A Woman's guide to living life on her terms. The soon to be published Author and Head Coach in the Academy, draws on her skills, depth & breadth of knowledge and experience gained in Corporate, where she built her reputation for her leadership ability at all levels. As a result, created her unique 'W.I.L.L Women Leadership Signature Programme' to provide Women with a step by step strategy to successfully go to the next level.

How to connect with me

www.facebook.com/astrid.phillips.52

www.instagram.com/i_am_coachastrid/

www.linkedin.com/in/astrid-phillips-award-winning-speaker-coach-and-mentor-8b57b787/

www.membby.com/coach-astrid/

I have a message just for you!
Scan me with your camera or QR app

WATCH NOW

Life after Rape

Chantal Ul Haq-Weedon

Rape.

Sitting here looking at that word on the page, it's hard to describe something when you don't really want to find the words. Unfortunately, rape happens, and many people are left paralysed and silenced, not knowing what to do next. If someone came to me today and said they'd been raped, I know the exact steps that I would take to support them and I hope to share this with you here. I am blessed enough to have a mum who took these steps for me, but not for a while because I couldn't find the words to tell her what had happened.

When I was raped, I had been so overpowered to the point that I couldn't speak up about what had just happened. I was 19 years old and was in my first year at Huddersfield University studying classical music. I was a confident young woman and I was looking forward to spending some time with a friend of mine from Uni who lived in London. I didn't drive at the time, so I travelled on the train and tube and was super excited because we were going to watch a film. I can't remember which one now.

At Uni, this guy was quiet but confident and came across as a genuine guy. He wasn't arrogant like some of the other guys at Uni and I had seen this appeal to several girls in my peer group. He actually had a girlfriend from London who would travel to stay with him a few times a month. This made me feel naively secure.

On this particular day, he picked me up at Ealing tube station, the closest stop to his house. He always dressed very well and today

was no exception. On the way to the house, we caught up on what had been going on since we saw each other the week before, laughing and joking about shenanigans that went on at Uni.

At the family home, there were two other male friends/family members there. He referred to them as 'cousins' but who knows if they were actually related. One of the 'cousins' was cooking, the house smelt of traditional Pakistani food. It was nice, but I later found out that it was also very spicy!

We all sat talking for a while, and even had some deeper conversations about religion. He and his cousins tried desperately hard to 'show me the way' and convert me to Islam. Being a strong headed young woman, I stood my ground and agreed that I respect other religions but my beliefs are strong and are unlikely to change.

We all had dinner and as the time went on I realised that we weren't going to watch a film after all. Everyone just sat either watching TV or chatting. I was slightly confused about not going out given that this was the actual reason for me going to visit.

I'd planned to stay over (in a non-romantic way) but as it didn't appear that we were actually going anywhere I asked for my overnight suitcase to be brought in from the car so I could get ready for bed. I was shown to my room, which appeared to be a guest bedroom.

I locked the door to get ready for bed, so you can imagine the surprise when my 'friend' walked in on me getting changed. Initially, I thought he was playing a prank but as he walked towards me, he looked at me in a way I'd never seen before. To say I felt petrified is an understatement. I'm not used to people, let alone a man, coming into my personal space. I remember trying to push

him away but I felt powerless. In that moment, I realised how young I still was, tears rolling down my face wishing I could go home to the safety of my parents. What he did that night will always be with me.

When he'd finished I lay there frozen, scared about what else would happen. He told me to get him a drink from the fridge downstairs. I was so traumatised about what had just happened, I probably would have done anything he told me to. I went downstairs, tears still streaming down my face. I walked into the kitchen, which was open plan with the lounge, to realise that one of his cousins was asleep on the sofa but one was still awake. He came over to me and he asked me if I was ok. After what had just happened I felt scared about what he might do. I'm sure he knew what had happened but I had no words. I didn't know if this cousin was a good man or a bad man. All I could say is 'he wants a drink'. He went to the fridge and got me a can of fizzy drink. As he stood in front of me, holding out the drink for me to take, I saw the way he looked at me, genuinely concerned. I just wanted him to help me but couldn't find the words to ask. I walked as slowly as I could upstairs, not wanting to return to the room. I handed the drink to him and stood there not knowing what to do. I had pain in my body and I just wanted to run away. He told me to get ready for bed and I remember being fearful of what that actually meant. I went to the bathroom and sat on the floor, hugging my knees and cried even more. I didn't want to make a sound so I turned on the shower and got in. I turned the water to as hot as I could take it on my skin. It stung as it was so hot but I had a feeling of it not being hot enough to clean me. I washed, and washed again. As I came out of the shower I saw how red my skin was. I stood in the bathroom, not knowing what to do next. If I called for help, I didn't know where I was. How would anyone find me? It wasn't like now where we have smart phones and GPS tracking.

I don't remember much more about that night but I do remember focusing on the sky outside and watching as the day began. I knew I couldn't sleep. It wasn't safe there. I was just desperate for the morning to arrive so I could ask to go home. I was dressed in my clothes ready to leave and had my bag packed by early morning. I refused breakfast and said I wanted to go home.

Before that night he had agreed to drive me home, so I wasn't travelling both ways on the train. Instead, he dropped me off at the station and threw £20 in my direction so that I could get home. In some way, I felt relief that I was no longer in his presence. But then I also felt betrayed and ashamed about what had taken place. Being thrown money like that made me feel like he'd paid me. Was that what my life was worth? That was the start of a low point in my life and a several months on an emotional rollercoaster. The last thing I remember was the car, a Honda Civic.

As I sat on the train, I was planning how to tell my mum what had happened the night before when she picked me up from the station. I was going over and over in my head, what I would say. I don't know if anyone saw me crying that day. I focused only outside and didn't allow myself to lock eyes with anyone. In that moment, everyone felt like the enemy, someone that I couldn't trust. I just had to get home.

It took over two hours to get home from Ealing to the south coast with train connections included. Once back in my hometown my mum had come to pick me up. I got into the family car and was still going over what I would say. I knew I had to say it now, otherwise it would be hard to say it at all.

Our dog had just been to the vets, my mum and brother were talking about the appointment. I got in and sat silently in the back seat and just like that, the courage to tell them had passed. I was

silent for the remainder of the car journey home, (only 5 minutes) but found comfort in the loving eyes of our dog. I think she knew something had happened as she looked deep into my eyes, as if she was asking me 'are you ok?' I held back the tears and stroked her fur as we shared a connection in time through silence.

I don't remember a lot about that first night back at home. I do remember laying in bed playing over the possibility that I could get pregnant from this monster of a man. I wasn't working at the time so the next morning I had to ask my brother for money to get the morning-after pill. It's not a conversation any sister should have to

unable to say why I needed it. I didn't want to go to the doctor

the pharmacist. My brother called a few different pharmacies to check they had it in stock. I was told I'd have to go into the pharmacy to speak to them before I could purchase it.

I had to sit there as they asked me personal questions about when I last had sex. I wish they knew it wasn't sex. I was so ashamed, sitting there, having to answer questions like it was normal for me to have sex, let alone unprotected! All these questions, but never the question that I needed them to ask (are you ok?). I took the tablet straight away and desperately tried not to think of what had happened. I think that made it worse. It was there, every second of every day. But I've never been so relieved for my period to start the next month.

I returned to Uni a few weeks later to begin the summer term. I was a broken person. I spent many days and nights crying, wishing I could talk to my family about it. I had a boyfriend at the time and he had a big heart. He lived in Nottingham and I'd met him through my flat mate at Uni. Although we didn't see each other often, he knew I was more distant than usual. I cried a lot but

couldn't explain to him why. He knew something was wrong and so pushed me until I eventually couldn't hold it back anymore. We had been arguing because I didn't want to say what had happened, I repeatedly told him he wouldn't understand, but my fear was also about this changing his view of me. I was scared that he would view me as dirty, as I felt, but that couldn't have been further from the truth.

We were stood in my room at Uni, he'd been repeatedly asking me what was going on. He thought my feelings for him had changed because I was being distance. He was epileptic and thought, goodness knows why, that maybe I'd changed my mind because of that. We were both extremely naïve. I broke down in front of him and told him I'd been raped. I could hear the anger in his voice, questioning if I meant I'd slept with someone. When I looked at him in that moment, he knew that was the worst thing he could have asked me. I panicked thinking he didn't believe me, I fell to the floor sobbing whilst he initially asked me so many questions about who did this and when did it happen, where did it happen. To make it worse, he knew of the man who did it and knew he hadn't returned to Uni that semester. He was understandably angry, I saw hatred in his eyes that I'd never seen before. I ended up having to calm him down too but to be able to tell someone, it brought relief. I wasn't going through this alone anymore. After the initial reaction, he held me, silently, and it felt good to know I wasn't alone. He was the first person I confided in, about 4 weeks after it had happened.

My boyfriend wasn't Christian, he was actually Sikh, but after being told what had happened he travelled to Huddersfield from Nottingham almost every weekend to come with me to church on Sundays. He wanted to ensure that I had the support I needed whilst I was at Uni going through life after rape.

He pushed me to confide in a friend from the Christian Union and she took me to speak to one of her elders in the church. I thought they would take the pain away but the words that flowed out of that elder's mouth were unreligious and severely damaged my relationship with God for a while. 'Your boyfriend isn't Christian, so God made that happen to punish you'. It was like someone had winded me. Could that really be true? Is that what God is really like, punishing his children to teach them a lesson? I was so confused about what the elder had said. I turned away from God that day and refused to go to church or Christian Union again. I felt anger towards God for allowing this to happen.

It took me over three years to even attempt to go to church. I still felt betrayed by God because of what the elder had said, even though the words were untrue. This was something I had to find out for myself, and set me on a journey to find my faith again. But that's a whole different story!

The flatmate that connected me to my boyfriend had been, at one point, a very close friend. Before the summer holidays I remember telling her what had happened. She stared right at me and told me to turn the light off as I leave. I felt rejected. She didn't believe me. My heart broke. What if others don't believe me? A handful of close friends now knew but I decided that day that I wouldn't tell anyone again.

It was now the summer between the first and second year of Uni. Unsurprisingly I didn't progress to the second year and was having to repeat my first year all over again. This alone made me feel embarrassed and worthless. Being at home meant time away from my boyfriend who had been a great support. I was unable to find the words to tell my family what had happened which made me feel very alone, I had been to a counsellor and asked her how to

tell my parents everything that had happened. The suggestion? Sit them down on the sofa and tell them "I want to tell you something, but after I've told you I'm going to walk out of the room and I don't want you to ask any questions when I come back in'.

What normal human being wouldn't have the typical "What? When? How? Who?" types of questions? I couldn't do that to my parents. So instead, I stopped going to counselling and resumed 'normal life'.

During that summer I had been to visit a friend of mine who knew about everything. He'd asked me to give him a call when I got home so he knew that I had arrived safely. It was nice to know that I had friends that were protective of me. On my journey home, my mum had messaged to say that she and dad wanted a discussion with me at some point but hadn't said what about. Part of me feared that it could be about the rape but then I thought 'how could they know that?' and then continued racking my brain all the way home.

When I arrived back at home, my mum presented me with 'the facts' that she had overheard my brother talking to a friend about me getting the morning after pill. Can I just add at this point that mum is a church minister! Mum has always said she was on autopilot, managing the situation as if it was someone who had approached her as a minister. But whatever she did at that time, was exactly what I needed. I had time to talk, whenever I was ready, and she also came with me to the hospital to go through all the tests. She did so much and I truly appreciated her actions during that time. I will be forever grateful that she was there for me.

Fast forward five years. I dropped out of Uni, worked full time for a while and then returned to a different Uni and a different course. This time I was studying at Buckinghamshire New University and

the degree was Music, Entertainment and Arts Management. During my final year, I received a Facebook message from a male stranger. Facebook tells you groups you're connected with so I could see that he was also a student at the same Uni as me. He said he's in my class, I responded quite sarcastically with 'we only have nine in my class with one male, and he's definitely not you!'. This situation, a male at the same Uni, felt too close to home for me.

He explained that he was looking for people that he could speak with so that he could develop his English language skills. From this message, we started talking and eventually met up. This man, who I have the privilege of calling one of my best friends along with his wife, is Muslim. I hadn't held a deep conversation with a Muslim man since I was raped. He invited me to his student house with four other Muslim men. There was no way I was going in there! Not again. So, we sat outside in my car and chatted until the early hours of the morning.

I shared my story with him and explained why I was hesitant. That night, he taught me a valuable lesson, that I had been tarring all Muslim men with the same brush. I hadn't even realised I was doing it. If he hadn't taught me that lesson that night, we may not have been connected as best friends for the last 12 years. Even more, I wouldn't have met and married my Muslim husband who lived, at the time, with my best friend at Uni.

If you ever feel the universe or God is pushing you to do something, just do it! That small message from a stranger, who later became my best friend, led to a complete change in my life direction and I can never thank him enough for this. Through him, I have been blessed with an amazing friend (his wife), the best husband I was certain I would never have, and a loving extended family around the world. What a blessing it is to be welcomed into

such a family with open arms.

Before we say goodbye, I want to share with you that memories of trauma can come back to haunt you years later. Eighteen years after being raped I thought I had 'dealt with it'. I attended a day called 'a spa day for your soul', my mum was going and I decided to book a ticket and tag along. During that day, a remarkably strong young woman attended to share some songs that she had written. Her songs showed the pain she had been through, and I later found out that she had been sexually assaulted whilst live on stage. Although I don't believe this went as far as rape, she had the strength to go to court, aided by the fact that she had video footage. One of her songs spoke to me that day and I sat there with tears streaming down my face. I felt the need to speak to her afterwards, to tell her that I was so proud of what she was doing, (going to court) and she was doing this for all the people out there that hadn't had the courage to seek justice. As we spoke, I could barely control myself I was truly sobbing. I was taken aback by how raw this still was.

I had been attending counselling for something unrelated and I explained what had happened at the spa day for your soul. I don't understand why it came up at that point, I'd been married 9 years by then, but for whatever reason, my feelings around the rape had finally decided to surface. I spoke openly with the counsellor about how I found the conversation difficult, and I didn't know how deep I could go with it. The counsellor allowed me to steer the conversation, to whatever felt natural, but did speak about the possibility of these feelings coming back again, maybe even stronger in the future, if I hadn't given myself the time and space to work through the pain.

We spent as many sessions going through that as felt natural and discussed how this had impacted our marriage. I didn't want to

accept that it may have actually had an impact on the intimate relationship with my husband. I had begun working on myself, doing a course about life and relationship coaching. Through this course, I realised that being raped had, in fact, had a massive impact. I just hadn't realised it.

It became clear to me during that course that I had particular behaviours around intimacy. I didn't feel able to be intimate, unless I'd had a shower first, I also had a particular position that I used as a defence mechanism to ensure that I always felt in complete control. This is something that I might be working on for the rest of my life, but eighteen years later, I have finally acknowledged that trauma can last a lifetime if you don't allow your body and emotions time to heal.

If you are ever unfortunate enough to need to support a loved one after being raped, please:

1. Give them a safe space to talk openly if they want to. Be aware that they may feel unable to speak to you and that's okay. When the time is right, they'll talk.

2. Don't force any counselling or therapy on them before they are ready to do the work. Yes, even if it is eighteen years later.

3. Ask if they want to go to the police. This is a massive step, extremely intrusive, and almost like you are re-living it again. If you are attending the police station really soon after this has happened, it's likely to be traumatic and a lot of support is required. But also remember, if they don't feel able, or want to go to the police, that is still okay. It has to be whatever that person feels is right for them.

4. Offer support at a health check so they don't have to go through that awful experience alone. The tests are for sexually transmitted diseases including Aids, so support really is important here, even if they know that you are just outside.

5. Remind them they are never alone and are truly loved.

When I look back at that night, I want to scream at my younger self for all the things I should have done. My brain shut down. I was completely paralysed. I didn't go to the police and a year later found out he had raped someone else. That's a guilt that I can never take away but from my own experience, I know not everyone feels able to go to the police, and they need to be reminded that whatever they choose, it is okay.

Rape is a subject that many do not speak about, but it's for us to speak up and be heard when we feel able to. No one has to go through anything alone. And remember, good things really can still come through trauma.

Author: Chantal Ul Haq-Weedon

A quirky fact about me: Chantal Used to do travel on the radio

What I do now: Chantal Ul Haq-Weedon is a lawyer, author, entrepreneur, speaker and course creator. She is a multi-passionate entrepreneur who creates and funs courses as 'done for you products' and group and 1-1 programs. Chantal's signature course helps aspiring female entrepreneurs who want to create, launch and sell their own course so that they can leave their 9-5.

Chantal went from newly qualified to partner within 2 years and believed this to be the 'dream'. However upon reaching partner level, she felt unfulfilled and lost in life. This inspired Chantal to create a program for women in the corporate field who are feeling unfulfilled as she did. Chantal draws on her own experience to help her clients find their passion, re-discover themselves, find their true calling in life, the time, location and financial freedom they crave but also helps them to have a massive impact on the world.

Chantal will also be offering retreats in 2021 for women who need help in choosing the right direction, and if face to face retreats are still not possible in 2021, a virtual one will be completed.

How to connect with me:

www.facebook.com/chantal.weedon

www.linkedin.com/in/chantal-ul-haq-weedon-625a249/

I have a message just for you!
Scan me with your camera or QR app

Little Pea...

Yasemin Akcakoca

I am going to meet Carmen. I met her when I walked away from my unhappy marriage of five years. An unhappy marriage that lead to bulimia, I can't eat, not even a little green pea. Even If I try to eat it, the little pea wants to come back out from my mouth, and it hurts my throat a lot. So little help from the psychiatrist, I am not healing, it's not happening, she is not reaching my trauma. I talk for an hour, she seems to be listening, and then I see her watching the clock. I feel down, because I know she's not been listening, and it's now time to go. Please lady, find the solution, stop checking that big white clock on the wall, just a little help, please! I should be able to talk to a stranger, to get it off my chest for a few hours after all, but I can't, and the little pea still wants to come out...

Clock lady psychiatrist is referring me to an Employment Centre for Mental Health, where I can try to keep the little pea in my stomach, to learn new skills for employment and therapy, from so many different therapists. There she is... Carmen... An American lady... Great! I can actually understand her because I watched Sesame Street every day with the kids that I looked after when I first arrived in England. Didn't you learn English from children's programs and books too? Carmen says she has worked with families of Vietnam veterans, I kind of felt my traumas were mild compared to theirs, look how much pain she has witnessed too. Do I tell her everything? Is she going to question my trauma? Is she going to think, "you call this a trauma?"

We're in therapy, and I'm watching and listening to them crying, I feel so heavy, I end up in tears and would run to the toilets, usually

Carmen follows me and brings me back to the group. Everything is coming out, emotions, past traumas and the little pea. Two years I was there, I learnt how to use the computer and I developed IT skills. I also turned my feelings into paintings through art therapy, and also had them analysed. There were still times I would run out of the groups crying and would be brought back to them if I wanted to be. Telling this part of my story was hard to do, but I knew I needed the pain to stop. So I carried on sharing my story.......

The first day after the wedding, a question from the Father Figure...."Come on then aren't you going to wash my feet? That's what Turkish wives do, don't they?" "I don't know where you have this information from, but no, they don't". There it goes, his mask has dropped, 6 months of having fun and receiving flowers before the papers are signed, to giving up my own identity, thinking what a wonderful man I am married to, but all he wants are his feet washed!! Bit by bit I am losing my soul, becoming a little kid who listens and obeys the Father Figure.

I am learning, I am learning hairdressing, pottery, photography, sewing, driving, even parasailing. Can't see the point of hanging behind a boat so you can see what the world looks like 400meters above, but, there I am learning that skill too, because Father Figure wants me to learn it, so I can fly others around to make money. Don't misunderstand me, I am hungry to learn all that Father Figure is teaching me, but telling me not to eat much, and not to socialise is literally killing me. I have to clean, put his dinner on the table on time. "You won't survive without me!" he says. He teaches, then he shouts, he will not apologise but instead, he buys presents, just hands me the presents, presents to keep me quiet, a bribe... that's what it is a bribe! "What did he do this time", my mum says after seeing the last present he gave me. "It's just a car, just a present mum, he loves me," I said.

That present came after leaving me in the cold for 6 hours. He had locked all the doors so I couldn't get in. It was December, I was in my pyjamas, locked out, all because I went out with the girls from work and came back a bit late, and because I walked in all happy telling him I had such a lovely night. I am now feeling so

Another day, here we go, he's home from work, the temperature in the room changes, I'm feeling scared. I couldn't iron today because I was not well, must be the effects of staying out in the cold a few nights before. He tells me to get up and iron, "it's only a temperature!" Yes, only 39.4 degrees! I can't even walk I have had enough.

I am leaving, I'm feeling so scared thinking it's a wild world out there, no one to protect me. Only now, I can drive, and I have a car, that present! All I wanted to hear was I am sorry Yasemin, I am sorry for leaving you in the cold that night, I am sorry for hitting you, I am sorry for calling you names, I am so sorry for imprisoning you, I am sorry for locking you indoors when I go to work, I am

the same time as I did. That's all I wanted to hear… not presents.

You made a mistake Father Figure, you made a big mistake leaving me in the cold for hours and hours, trying to buy my pain with the car. This time you are not able to buy my pain, I will no longer live in constant fear. Yes!! I can drive! I am driving further and further away, the further away I drive the less I shake from fear. My temperature is still high, but do I care, no, I am leaving, I

My wings are so weak, but I will try my best… I am out there in the wild world, feeling the fear, heading to my only relative, Uncle Rene, my dad's stepbrother. I arrive, I'm safe, I made it! I have

somewhere to stay at least... Where I don't have to prepare dinner and serve on time. Somewhere where I'm not being hit, where I'm free to walk around the house without fear of being imprisoned. Somewhere where I am respected and loved for being ME. It's not bad here, Uncle Rene can't stop the pea leaving my body, and he leaves me to it. I'm starting to feel settled.

Oh No, why can't he leave me alone. Father Figure comes to my uncle's door with a bunch of flowers, he is saying sorry, what! he is saying sorry! He is crying, begging me to come home. How dare he come to the house that he didn't allow me to go near for 5 years, I wasn't allowed, in case I would talk and maybe someone would save me, oh no I wasn't allowed, how dare he come here.

I stayed with Uncle Rene, we had fun, for a while at least, God didn't I miss having a good laugh. However, I know it's a distraction, I'm hiding from my feelings, the pain, the hurt Father Figure caused, and I have stopped eating. When Uncle Rene comes home from work, we laugh, but I cannot eat, even if I force myself, it all comes out again. I don't tell Uncle Rene much, I wear my fake brave smile, he doesn't know I can't eat, he doesn't know the pea keeps coming out. I keep it a secret, I think I am depressed, and it feels like I am on my own and suffering.

My health started to get worse and on one particular day I nearly got run over by a car, because I couldn't cross the road safely, I was hungry, weak, depressed and shaking, the driver was shouting at me, I can't cope, I can't go on like this.

That's when I decided I needed help. That's when the lady psychiatrist looking at the big white clock comes into my life. One hour of hmmm, really, oh dear, and then? That's all I got from those sessions, I remember her words all the time, "time is up, see you next week" Chop Chop… as I'm hurried out the door! But I

have so much to talk about lady! Sorry, we only have an hour a week and only for 8 sessions. Oh yeah, 25 years will be sorted in 8 hours. Ok, you professionals know best.

I Left Uncle Rene's and I am now in a bedsit, a room in an attic and it's very hot here... I can still go and see him and have our laughs, but I am still in such a dark place and I don't really want to bother anyone, I feel like a burden, I could not even keep the tablets in my tummy. I was aiming to kill myself, it all came out, and that's when I was referred to the centre by the big white clock lady. Thank you, lady!

Therapies, followed by more therapies, although now I can recognise emotions and I know where they are coming from, which makes it easier to deal with, I'm sorting out the traumas and I'm getting good at it actually. I now know why I was married to a Father Figure, why I cannot hold that little pea in my tummy, it's because the Father Figure didn't want me to eat much, so I wouldn't be the big fat girl next to him. Five years of teaching me life skills as a father would, but at a price.

My hunger for learning is still there, I have always enjoyed computers and painting, and now I am also socialising with friends from the centre. I am starting to heal, I am enjoying Carmen's groups, and this is where everything comes out. Look at me Father figure, my issues are being sorted out! I am getting stronger I am safe here.

A few of my heroes in the centre want to talk to me as they are worried, they are saying they don't want me to become institutionalised. What does that mean? I have to go and check that word in my dictionary after the meeting. Ah yes, I understand, they care, two years now so they want to see me moving on. They don't want to see me get institutionalised in this place. Am I ready?

Am I able to fly by myself? I have been keeping the pea in me for a while now, I am making progress. I must be ready, but I also need to look for work, I am scared to leave this place, I am scared to leave the security, the learning, I am scared to leave.

Carmen, she is my hero. She is a solid human being who knows everything about feelings and how to deal with them, and she knows everything about me, she knows my pain and we talk outside the group from time to time, during one to one therapy. She is so strong, oh god, she isn't becoming a mother figure, is she? Can't be.

I am learning to bring out every emotion and dealing with them because Carmen is teaching me that, she is teaching me to say no. It's ok to say no.

I am also talking to her about my family overseas, why I left them, how I feel guilty for leaving them. I was the father to my brothers after my dad left us all, and we talked about how I had a life full of dramas and traumas, and how I had to grow up so quickly to take care of my brothers from a very young age. She is teaching me how to deal with guilt and I am learning.

Knowing that I am a qualified hairdresser and that she trusts me, Carmen asked me to perm her hair. It is Short, silvery grey hair, I can do it! Yes, I can, I believe in myself. We are not going to tell anyone in the centre, after its closed, that's when we are going to have our girly hairdressing session. All sorted. I borrowed some perm rollers and lotion from Uncle Rene's hairdressing salon. Yes, Uncle Rene is a hairdresser too.

Carmen and I are chatting away, and I am putting the rollers in her hair, her hair has to be perfect. I am so happy to spend extra time with Carmen and every word that comes out from her mouth is

treasured by me. She is telling me about herself now and how she fell in love with the man who brought her to England.

The more she talks, the more upset she is getting. Carmen is telling me how she is not happy, she is not happy with her life. She is now shaking, shaking and crying, she is so sad. I don't know what to say really, I keep putting the rollers in and listening to her, acknowledging her pain. All that crying and getting it all off of her chest, she clearly needed to do that.

All Carmen wants is to go to Ireland, find a country house and write her book. That's Carmen's dream. I am telling her to go for her dreams. She can do it. Look at me I am telling Carmen to follow her dreams! Beautiful lady you are Carmen. You have no idea how you changed my life for the better.

After apologising for talking about her sorrows, and me reassuring her that it was ok, we carried on talking, it made me realise that we all have problems, even Carmen, I am not alone, no-one is, life is not perfect, not even Carmen's. We all have stories to tell, feelings to deal with and It's ok to cry It's, ok to share. Her hair looks beautiful, I am so proud of myself, washed, blow-dried and she looks so good and feels good too.

Within a week I am out there starting my new job working as a stylist and working full time and visiting the centre every opportunity I get.

Every person we meet has an impact on our lives.

Thank you Father Figure for saying sorry with a car.

Thank you, Uncle Rene, for keeping me safe, and for the laughter.

Thank you big white clock watching lady psychiatrist for referring me to the centre where I met Carmen.

Thank you, Carmen, for healing me patiently, thank you for helping me to keep the little pea in my tummy, thank you for making me realise that I am a human being and all the feelings are ok, as long as you know how to deal with them. Thank you for making me realise that I am not alone. You helped me to grow and I am hoping that I have given something back to you all in return.

Big thank you, I love you all.

Author: Yasemin Akcakoca

A quirky fact about me: English is my second language, however my dreams are in English, no subtitles ☺

What I do now: Yasemin is the Director of her own business called AYA Retreats Ltd. Organising bespoke holistic retreats in Turkey, that bring diverse groups together in beautiful surroundings to enjoy wonderful experiences that nurture our mind, body and soul.

Yasemin is currently studying NLP (Neurolinguistic Programming) and working towards a Master Herbalist Diploma. She is a qualified Reiki Healing Specialist.

How to connect with me:

www.facebook.com/yasemin.akcakoca.5/

www.Instagram.com/yasemin1964/

www.linkedin.com/in/yasemin-akcakoca-98181648

I have a message just for you!
Scan me with your camera or QR app

Diary of a Single Professional Mum!

Kath Wynne-Jones

Have you ever heard of the phrase a woman's intuition?

25th May 2019: It's 3am and I'm standing against the aged wooden kitchen unit, clutching a crystal tumbler filled with brandy. I can feel the cold slate floor underneath my feet. Is it the last glass of the night before or the first of the day?

The kitchen is a mess, broken glass and crockery everywhere. The room is a mess, my life is a mess and I'm a mess.

Just hours prior, the atmosphere was so different. We were getting ready for our annual camping trip with our friends. Me and my beautiful daughter Emma were singing excitedly to One Direction, whilst we were packing our things. She was getting together her clothes, her beauty products and her fake tan, whilst I was packing the snacks, the food and most importantly the wine and the gin! You know one of those times where you think you're going for a month rather than a week, with the amount of stuff that you pack!

And then it all changed...

My husband of 21 years, about 5 ft 9, bald head and a beard entered the room.

"Kath we need to talk. We're not going on holiday tomorrow". "What, of course we're going on holiday, I've spent all night packing the campervan". "No, we're not going on holiday" as he gestures his finger between the 2 of us. "But, but I don't understand... What, what are you trying to tell me?" "Kath, I'm sorry, I'm telling you that this isn't working, and I want a separation

At the top of my voice, I am shouting and sobbing “Sorry, sorry, what do you mean you’re sorry! I’ve been saying for ages that things weren’t right and we needed to sort stuff out, and you kept telling me it was all in my head, and now you’re telling me you want to separate. I don’t understand, I just don’t understand.

Why couldn’t you have been honest with me sooner?
What are we going to tell Emma?
How am I going to cope on my own?
What are we going to tell our friends?
What are we going to tell our parents?
Was it all my fault? I just don’t understand… “

Have you ever had a time when you have known that in an instant your life has changed?

Before I knew it, I had shattered everything in the kitchen - the plates, the crockery, and the glasses. I was filled with rage in a way I have never been in my entire life before. This was totally out of character for me, as I am normally a very quiet, calm and peaceful person.

The thing was, I wasn’t really angry at him, well I was a bit… I was angry at myself. I was angry at myself for how long, and how often I had contained my sense of knowing something wasn’t right. I was angry at the small things I’d ignored, something that wasn’t right in a friendship or problems at work. And I was really angry at the big things I had ignored, the fact I knew I was losing myself for many years that led me to an emotional breakdown, and the fact I knew there was something wrong in my marriage, but I didn’t know how to deal with it.

Have you ever had a time in your life when everything appears broken in front of you, and you have no idea how to rebuild it?

September 19th 2019: I'm at a beautiful barn in Huddersfield on my latest personal development course – the Find Your Why Masterclass. For years I've been searching trying to find my true purpose in life. I know I'm here to make a difference, but I don't know what that looks like. The sun is streaming through the windows, I'm sat on the brown leather sofa clutching a cup of coffee, and I can hear the babbling brook at the bottom of the garden. Cheryl is stood opposite me, pen poised on the flip chart. She's laughing, her blonde hair in plaits, and her glasses pushed to the end of her nose. Marion is sat next to me, her legs crossed underneath her, looking as though she is about to start one of her meditation sessions. I can feel her positive energy reaching out to me. Both of these people have been a huge support and inspiration to me over recent weeks, but still, all I can see in front of me is that I am a failure…

In the style of Jeremy Paxman, Cheryl is interrogating me about my successes, but I'm not really seeing many.

"Right, come on the Kath, you are a Director in the NHS. You must have overcome some challenges to succeed in your career". "Err... yep ok. I probably have done some stuff I'm proud of…"

"Well I used to work excessive hours and was constantly connected to my emails and my phone, because it was the only place I got any self-worth. I had a nervous breakdown in 2016, which made me re-evaluate things. Now I know I do a good job, I'm more productive and have a good work-life balance".

"Ok, what else?"

"Err.. I've completed a marathon and a couple of triathlons. And I've got enough professional certificates to decorate the downstairs of my house. When I commit to something, I will put all my effort

into it to achieve what I set out to do. I've got a brilliant relationship with my daughter, and I know I have friends and family who care about me"

Cheryl writes down the topics I have told her.

Work
Achievements
Relationships

"So Kath, what can you see in front of you? What's the common connection?"
"Erm, me…?" "Yep, no shit Sherlock. What else?"

As I studied closer, the word WAR appeared in front of me. I realised I had been at WAR with myself my entire life. Tears rolled down my cheeks, nothing I ever did was good enough by my standards, I was always onto the next thing, the next qualification, the next promotion, the next event. I had never stopped to celebrate my accomplishments or to appreciate that I was a good, kind person, without all of that.

I was grateful for everybody and everything in my life, but I didn't value myself at all. My resilience was strong, to keep going with everything, but my levels of joy and my self-esteem were at rock bottom.

October 14th 2019: From the time my marriage ended, I knew this day was coming. The day I had been dreading. The day I face my biggest fear. The anxiety in my body has been building all week, and I'm not proud of how I reacted to Emma this morning, as I felt less in control of my emotions than normal. Getting irritated at her about being late for school, and her not having packed her bags

quickly enough. None of this was her fault. It was because I couldn't manage my insecurities well enough. It's my first night away from Emma since the separation. She is staying at her Dad's new house for the first time, and it's the first day I find myself truly alone.

For as long as I can remember, I have always feared being on my own, but never really understood why. Today I understand. I am able to name my fear, and my reality of being abandoned by my partner. I feel alone, isolated and like I have nobody in the world who is by my side. From being very young, I never felt like I fitted in. I was always the odd one out at school. I had quite a lonely childhood as an only child. I wasn't really invited to play with others, and I didn't have the confidence to join in myself. The brass band circle, where I met my husband, had accepted me. When I joined the Band, I felt like at last I belonged somewhere and with someone, which made our separation even harder, as I felt like I had lost everything that helped me to feel secure, and gave me a sense of belonging.

After my realisation at the Find Your Why Headquarters, of how much at WAR I have been with myself, I am now trying to treat myself with compassion, kindness and care. It can be a challenging process when you've lived with a crazy flatmate in your head for 43 years. Quietening her negative voice is not happening overnight, but I am making small strides to speak kindly to myself and see the positive opportunities in difficult situations. As I work my way through this marital separation to the best outcome for us all, I am constantly faced with the light and dark sides of change.

Sometimes I feel the changes day to day, sometimes I feel them hour to hour, and sometimes I feel them minute to minute, depending upon external things that are happening, my state of

mind, and the support I have around me. I am holding onto the fact that I can only face the light if I live in the dark for a while. I know there are always two sides of change. Lots of people have been telling me that writing will help me to heal, I'm not sure if I'm honest, but here goes with my first blog:

Why me?
This happened for a higher purpose that will one day become clear to me

I need to control everything to get through this
Where do I need to put my trust and faith to get me through this?

I don't understand what's going on
I don't have to understand what's going on – one day I will understand why this happened

I'm weak and I can't get through this
This experience will make me a stronger more resilient person

It's all my fault, and I'm mad and angry at myself for not being a different person, to be able to make this relationship work
I am enough, I have good qualities and it takes 2 for a relationship to fail

I'm angry at the situation and I don't deserve this
What lessons does the universe feel I need to learn through and from this experience?

Why is no one else in my family feeling the same amount of pain, is it because they don't care?
Everybody has their own process – it doesn't mean they don't care but everyone has their way of dealing with things

How will this ever be OK?
It will be ok in the end, if it's not ok, it's not the end

13th December 2019: I'm stood on a 6ft wide red velvet circle, with a 10ft red glitter shoe to the right of me, the big red letters T.E.D. to the left to me, and what seems like thousands of people facing me in the audience. I am approaching the last few minutes of my TEDx talk on Resilience, and sharing what I believe from my own research and education are the 3 key factors of Resilience.

"I believe the 3 F's of Resilience are:

1. Your Feelings:
Noticing and accepting your feelings whether they be good or bad. If we suppress negative emotions, they can make us ill. If we don't take time to reflect on the big and small positive things that happen in our lives, they can sometimes pass us by.

2. Your Focus:
Putting your focus on the future, and what you can do to change your mental state if you find you are in a funk. For me, I know that going for a run, even though I may not always want to do it, will almost always make me feel better. What is it that you do that changes your emotional state?

3. Your Friendships:
Who are the people you can go to who accept you unconditionally, will not judge you, and inspire you to become the best you can be? Are you prioritising those people, or are you focusing on what the people who drain your joy say to you? The best piece of advice someone gave me was if you won't go to someone for advice, don't listen to their criticisms.

I believe resilience is like the Japanese art of Kintsugi. When

pottery breaks, it's not thrown away, it's threaded by gold to mend it and make it more beautiful. I believe as a human being, each one of the challenges we face is represented by a crack in the pottery. Each time we overcome a challenge we become more beautiful and resilient human beings."

The audience are clapping and cheering, and I am overcome with a sense of pride that I have never felt in my life before. The happiest day of my life was the day that Emma was born, closely followed by my wedding day, but I couldn't take sole responsibility for my happiness on either of those occasions. Today I am proud of me, and I know that the sense of satisfaction I have is a result of the effort I have put in to start to recreate my life positively.

I could so easily have still been crying on the kitchen floor with a bottle of wine, but instead, I knew I had to grow as a person to be a positive role model to my daughter and others. Now, don't get me wrong, it hasn't been an easy journey over the past 6 months. There have been many days when I have cried, looked for answers that aren't there, asked myself what did I do wrong, was it my fault or was it because I had a career? None of these were helpful questions, but it has taken many different people who believed in me, when I didn't believe in myself, to build my confidence and momentum, to help me ask myself these useful questions.

31st December 2019: My diary entry as I sit on the balcony of our skiing chalet in Chamonix looking out towards Mont Blanc.

Dear 2019, you were interesting…

- You gave me a divorce and the associated heartbreak, loneliness, guilt, shame and unworthiness that went with it

- You gave me struggles as a leader to believe I was not having any beneficial impact on people's lives
- You enabled me to connect at a deeper level with my daughter and friends in a way I didn't think possible
- You provided me with an opportunity to travel with Emma and my friends and experience new parts of the world. If you had told me I would be going on our family holiday to Lanzarote on my own with Emma, and was going to have the most amazing time ever, or that I would be in Dubai coaching people to be a better version of themselves, I wouldn't have believed you
- You supported me in becoming an ACE Mentor, TEDx Speaker and to share what I am passionate about in the world
- As Emma and I have settled into our new life, I have felt life return to me. I feel alive, that I have opportunities in front of me that I can do or be anything I want to be

I am thankful for this year because…

- You didn't just hand me a separation from my husband. You helped me feel whole on my own, though this is an ongoing journey
- You didn't make me lose hope in love
- You didn't overwhelm my family with trauma
- You've helped me to start to express myself
- You've guided me to people, support and communities who will help me grow
- You've let me experience new things, with many more to come in 2020
- You've helped me to love and accept myself and those around me in a way that I never could before

In 2020, I want to:

- Express myself fully
- Be the best mum I can be to Emma and my doggies
- Take full responsibility for my mental, physical, emotional and spiritual health by putting in place healthy daily habits
- Spend time with friends doing things that don't cost lots of money, and feed my body, mind and spirit (New insert: little did I know that would be on Zoom every Saturday night because there's nowhere else to go!)
- Travel to new parts of the world
- Become a best selling author, world-class speaker, start my own business and launch my online products and events
- Focus on being in the present and enjoying the now, rather than living in the past or the future
- Be the best leader I can be, by spending my time and energy in places where I can have a positive impact
- Create a home environment that supports me and Emma emotionally, physically and spiritually
- Create opportunities for joy, fun and expressing my creativity each day

Goodbye, 2019! x

January 25th: Swipe right, swipe left – this is a whole other world! Quite frankly this online dating world could be another full-time job, that I'm not sure I am ready for. I think I am reacting to the fact that my ex-husband has a new girlfriend, but I know there is no way I'm ready for another relationship. My confidence in myself is growing, but I don't think I can handle the brutality of the online dating world just yet! I realise that I need time on my own, time to heal, and time to start believing in myself, trusting myself and loving myself, knowing that a new partner will appear when the time is right.

April 18th 2020: Today would have been my 22nd wedding anniversary. I should have been in Amsterdam today (escaping if I'm honest!), but instead, I am in the Boardroom of the Hospital. My anxiety levels are through the roof with the emotions of the day, and this being my 5th week of 12 hour days 5 days a week in the hospital, trying to be a good mum, supporting home-schooling, not knowing really how to switch off, and feeling challenged with everything that COVID is presenting me with.

My COVID experience is different to many of my other friends. It hasn't been a time for reflection. It's been a time for working really hard and trying to support the NHS in the best way I can. I am grateful for the Thursday night clap and seeing my neighbours. I am grateful for friends who have brought me wine, chocolates and flowers, and I am grateful for the fabulous team I work with.

But if I'm honest, my head is spinning trying to balance the different responsibilities of life. I'm feeling a little envious of not being able to press the pause button, and I am really struggling facing into the emotions of the fact that I am not celebrating our wedding anniversary, but I know that this too shall pass.

May 3rd 2020: About a week ago, I realised how tired I was, and how disconnected I'd become in those relationships that are important to me. Over recent weeks, due to work and home pressures, I've sacrificed my morning routine, in favour of other things – notably scrolling through Facebook late at night and first thing in the morning, which is not adding any value to my life.

Normally my daily routine is:

- Wake up and write my gratitude diary at 6am
- Meditate for 30 minutes

- Get ready for work
- Have a glass of water, my vitamins and my breakfast before I go to work
- Make sure the dogs and Emma are sorted

And if I've got a later meeting, maybe do some form of exercise too.

A week after setting my morning routine back in place, and doing the things that keep me well, I am feeling so much better, and I know this has to be my priority to enable me to be there for others.

What is it that you need to do for yourself to keep you well, so that you are making you a priority?

Kindness is the theme for mental health awareness week this month. There has been so much kindness shown across our communities in recent weeks and months, which I hope will long continue. People are shopping for each other, taking the time to ring or Facetime people who are on their own, lending technology so that people can stay connected, donating food and other items to those who need it.

In my health and care organisation, I have seen so many moving stories of people and teams going above and beyond, to give compassionate care to patients and service users. Teams are coming together across organisations and working together in ways that we could have only dreamed of 12 months ago. Through this pandemic, there has been more collaboration across teams and organisations, than I have ever seen in my career before in the NHS, because we have all been working to one purpose.

I have been humbled by how people working across health and social care nationally, have continued to deliver great care for our

population and helped to save lives, despite the challenges of home-schooling, uncertainties around household incomes, and the loneliness that themselves, friends or family may have been facing. Despite the tragedy of this pandemic, I hope that the positive new ways of delivering care, and that the spirit of gratitude, compassion and kindness remains long after the lockdown. Amid fear, there is also community, support and hope.

I'm not sure things will ever return to 'normal' either in our personal or professional lives. However, as shoots of life Pre-COVID start to appear, what are the positive things that you will be keeping in your life?

For me, I now shop weekly and prepare most of our meals, rather than running into the supermarket every couple of days, which has impacted positively on me reconnecting with my home, having a better diet, and spending time with my daughter .

20th June 2020: I can see the waves lapping against the sea wall, a wave boarder is trying to ride the huge waves, the sun is setting in front of us, and I am sat with Emma in our little black Mini in Blackpool. The smell of Harry Ramsden's fish and chips is filling the car, and we're singing along to One Directions 'Up All Night'.

I feel at peace with everything that has happened, and positive about opportunities that life is presenting me with. 5 days ago my decree nisi was passed through court. The weekend before the decree nisi was passed I cleared the loft, (which hadn't been sorted for 20 years), of things that I was hanging onto, that were keeping me stuck in the past.

I donated all of Emma's old baby things to charity. I had kept everything in the loft, in the hope that I got pregnant again, but It wasn't meant to be. Emma is the most wonderful daughter that I

could ever wish for, but I didn't want her to be an only child, as I didn't want her to experience the loneliness I had as a child. These past few months have taught me that my experience is not hers. She is not lonely with her best friend Zoe living across the road, and the beautiful friendship group she has at school. Emma's now fourteen, and I'm forty-four. I think it's probably time to say goodbye to the sterilisers, baby grows and the guilt that I have been carrying, of being unable to give Emma a brother or sister.

I sorted out childhood memories into boxes for the 3 of us to keep. As I sorted through all our things, I reflected on the happy times we had experienced as a family, expressed sadness that we were no longer a family unit, but expressed deep gratitude for the times we had spent together going on holidays, celebrating birthdays and doing the small things like feeding the ducks or going to the park.

I carefully boxed up all the old photographs and family memories together for Emma when she is older, as this was a joyful part of our lives that I don't want to pretend didn't happen, even though things are different now.

Today as I sit in front of the sea, I am happy. My eyes are filled with happy tears, as I feel my life filled with joy. I am spending time with the most precious person in my life, and I am proud of myself for overcoming the challenges I have faced. I have sorted lots of practical stuff like the divorce, the remortgage, refurbishing the house to make it my own, and most importantly being able to configure the Wi-Fi and connect the Sonos speaker.

I have formally launched my coaching business, and I'm using my knowledge, skills and experience through my creation of 'The Blissful Leadership Blueprint', to help others who may be facing difficult times in their life too.

But most importantly, I have learnt how to accept things as they are, know that everything is as it should be and that the best is yet to come. If it's not OK, it's not the end.

I have learned to put my faith in something bigger than myself, and to lean on other people for support. I know that I am blessed with the best set of friends that a girl could wish for. I am practicing how to take control of my mind and my emotions.

Over the last 12 months, I have discovered that being a woman is not about being at WAR with yourself or others. I believe it's about being RAW. It's about being Real, Authentic and Wise. It's about showing up as you and always trusting your intuition to guide you on the right path.

I hope that my reflective diary may give you some comfort or inspiration if you are facing challenges in your life.

Always keep in your heart one of life's famous quotes:

"The greater the storm the brighter the rainbow"

Author: Kath Wynne-Jones

A quirky fact about me: I have performed in a Burlesque Dance Show

What I do now: I am a leader in Health and Social Care, a Coach, Mentor, Teacher, Tedx Speaker, Entrepreneur and mostly a Mum to my amazing daughter Emma. I help people to live their life authentically with purpose, joy and resilience. Using experience and innovative tools and techniques, I guide people to take responsibility for leading an international life, to help to grow compassionate families, communities and workplaces. At the core of my work, is helping clients to develop a positive an inner connection with themselves, to be guided by their own intuition.

How to connect with me:

www.facebook.com/kath.wynnejones.9

www.linkedin.com/in/kath-wynne-jones-leader-coach-tedx-speaker-7a828859/

@kathwj

I have a message just for you!
Scan me with your camera or QR app

Live the life you love

Jodie Lee Liggett

Wow! It is actually happening.....

Do you ever chat about things you'd love to do *one day*?. But never make any real plans to make them happen. These might be things like; taking a hot air balloon ride, visiting a relative in America, seeing the pyramids in Egypt, canoeing down the river Thames, writing a book maybe, living by the sea or taking your kids to Disneyland?

You may sometimes sit there daydreaming when you get a quiet moment, but then reality kicks in, or maybe it is logic that is getting in the way, maybe you think to yourself, there's no time for that, the kid's schoolwork is a priority at the moment, they need a steady routine. Money is tight, we can only stretch to essentials right now. I need to concentrate on work, I have loads of responsibilities here, people are relying on me.

You may find all sorts of reasons to justify putting these dreams off, but are they really reasons, or are they excuses? If you knew you had a limited time to live, how would that change your priority list? It is an interesting question to consider isn't it? We don't know how much time any of us have left to live, all we really have is now.

Let me tell you "whatever you think you can or cannot do is true." As the great Henry Ford quote states. Many times, we stay tied to doing what we have always done, going from day to day, not realising that years are passing us by slowly but surely, and the dreams stay unlived in our heads.

You might be one of these people who don't even dare to dream! Because there is no point, dreams are for fairy tales, and not real life. I would like to challenge you to be open and listen to my story, and by the end of it reassess what is possible in your reality.

Are you living from your head or your heart? Is one better than the other?

I want to go back to 2017, it had been a tricky year for me. I was dealing with the aftermath of some traumatic events that took place in 2016. I had been left heartbroken for several reasons, which felt extremely painful emotionally. I then developed a kind of numbness in my heart which happened automatically, I guess it was the best I could do to cope. I knew this lack of emotion was not good for me in the long run.

After some time being shut off, my emotions were stirred up again when my ex-boyfriend got in touch. We met up and my heart let in a flood of feelings, I let myself be vulnerable, it was a risk for sure, but I was happy I could feel something.

I realised that in our relationship and all the relationships I had ever experienced, my heart had never been fully open, I had put up a guard. Seeing this guy again had caused me to re-think and I decided I wanted to stop doing that from now on. This situation with my ex was complicated though. Somehow, I now found myself wrapped up in a love triangle. It all felt like a bit of a messed-up game, one which deep down went completely against my personal values. Really, I'd rather not be involved in that kind of thing. This situation continued on and off for a long time, into 2018. I needed to get some self-respect!

I decided I needed to do something about it, but what? I went to see a friend who works with energy. I told her a little bit about my predicament and shared how I was feeling extremely anxious and stuck, and didn't know what to do. To be completely honest I felt a bit desperate. I wanted to help myself feel better, but I kept longing for the fix to come from someone else. I longed to feel wanted and I thought that if I was wanted that would make me feel happy. I felt the opposite though, sadness and a great fear of being rejected.

My friend and I spoke about this and rather than focus on the stuff I couldn't change, or continue to hang around waiting for this guy to make up his mind, hoping that he would come back to me, my friend suggested something else.

"Do something for you" she said. "Treat yourself, think of something you can do that you will look forward to."

The theory I guess would be for me to gain back a feeling of empowerment, an enjoyment that could be created by myself. It would be something unrelated to the situation that was bringing me down……. I had a think …… That was when I remembered, years ago I had wanted to climb Mount Snowdon.

Not quite a pamper day or getting my nails done, but something I felt was much better than that! It's time to live my dreams. I thought, "YES that is it! I am going to climb Mount Snowdon."

Just making that decision got me really excited, I knew in that moment something inside of me had shifted and I felt very certain and in control of making it happen. I could see how much meaning

it would hold, in a physical way it would be a great achievement, but also metaphorically, I knew this would represent something huge, overcoming obstacles and really proving to myself that I can achieve whatever I put my mind to.

I thought back to when the dream of climbing Mount Snowdon first came about. A group of us were out walking in the woods, most of my family were there, me and a friend of my Mum's where chatting. He was telling me about his adventures in Wales and how beautiful the scenery was. He had climbed Mount Snowdon before and wanted to go again.... I was excited hearing his story, and I loved the idea of doing it myself one day. He said "we should all go." My sister and her children were in, they wanted to go to Wales too, and so did my Mum, I remember my daughter asking "is daddy going to come?" I remember her asking that very clearly. Back then she was excited about the idea too. I was imagining the whole bunch of us going and thinking "it's going to be great." Little did any of us now when we were talking that afternoon in the woods, that both my daughters Dad, and my Mum could not possibly come along when we finally did make the journey.

So many twists and turns have happened in my life between having that chat in the woods and the decision to make it happen for real, five long eventful years had passed.

The Christmas of 2018 felt just as empty as many recent Christmases had, and as we moved into January, the prospect of moving away from that bleak feeling in my heart gave me hope. I knew things were changing, I had decided they were. That discussion with my healer friend was one of the things that made me feel really motivated, along with being really pleased that I had

signed up to start a spiritual training course that I would be studying throughout the coming year.

Although I found myself in mid- winter, which was out of season for tourism, I didn't care about that, I had plans to make, and this trip was going ahead no matter what.

Booking just after the festive season actually worked out well for us, because there was a January sale on the YHA (Youth Hostel Association) website, meaning there was plenty of availability, and with the discount I could afford to book us a private room rather than stay in a communal dormitory. I enjoyed researching about the different paths and apparently the Miner's Track would be suitable for kids. There was a hostel right across the road! The next school holiday was approaching so I made our reservation for the coming February half term.

I couldn't help but think back to the previous year. My daughter and I had spent half term with my sister and family at a UK holiday resort using tokens from the Sun newspaper. I reminisced, my sister travelled up in one car full of kids and supplies. My daughter, one of her cousins and me travelled in Grandad Colins car. It was so cold that year, we had to take hot water bottles to bed and leave the radiators on full blast all day.

Our lakeside log cabin was idyllic, when the snow began to fall it seemed magical, and especially perfect for the onsite dry ski slope. The snow got heavier though and there were weather warnings! Not so idyllic! Our stay had to be cut a short, everything closed down and we all got evacuated, it was either that, or risk getting snowed in. It took some time to pack up all of our things, I remember Grandad Colin and me rushing, while my sister leisurely

carried on playing outside with the kids, which meant we probably left a bit later than was advisable, but all added to the adventure! The snow was getting even heavier and by the time we reached the motorway on the way home it was that thick it settled on roads while traffic was driving along at high speeds! The cars ground to a halt and we got stranded on the motorway for 6 hours or more as the blizzard got worse. This was the snow-storm they named 'Beast from the East', luckily, we had blankets and supplies of food and drink. No one knew how long we would be stuck there! I remember feeling like we were in a sci-fi film!

Now as I made arrangements for the Wales trip of 2019, I remember thinking to myself this year would be different. 'The weather will be fine, it is completely possible to have lovely sunshine in February, IT WILL BE HOT THIS YEAR.' I went ahead and booked the hostel with absolute confidence it would all work out perfectly.

As the big day approached, I considered the drive I'd have to make from London to Wales, the longest drives I had ever taken before were between 2 and three hours long. Concentrating and finding my way to somewhere completely new for a minimum of four hours was the one thing, if any, that I was a bit apprehensive about, could I do it? My answer was *" I'll have to!"* Mostly I was excited!

The bags were packed, phones charged, and we had a full tank of fuel in the car (it's not very often that happens). The half-term holidays had begun, and we were on our way to Wales! I remember hearing 'Giant' by Rag n Bone man on the radio for the first time as we zoomed along the motorway. Something about that song lit me up inside. *"Now I'm strong enough for both of us, stand up on my shoulders, tell me what you see? I AM TRYING".*

Immediately I loved it, although later when I found out the real lyrics, I realised, I had been making up some of my own for a while, completely unaware of the song title.

My daughter, who was 11 at the time, had her friend and a cousin along for the adventure as well. I was delighted she had company her own age, because being a tween (pre-teen) is a time of life when it is very UNCOOL to hang out with your Mum (apparently). However, I was still the butt of their entertainment quite a lot of the time. They found it particularly amusing when I talked about how rocks have energy. I still hear jokes about the rocks and their energy to this day!

We made one stop half way to Wales for slush puppies and the toilet, then arrived pretty much within the estimated four hours, it was perfect. Along the way, I was in awe as we got deeper into the welsh landscape. The natural beauty was breathtaking, I just kept thinking ‘this is a dream come true’.

I always liked this quote.
“Mountains Gandalf, I want to see mountains“
(by Bilbo Baggins; Lord of the Rings J.R.R. Tolkien)

Even the kids seemed excited when we appeared to be in the midst of a hay storm as we followed a farm supply truck slowly around some windy hilltop roads. The car was again buzzing with laughter as we raced alongside what appeared to be clouds, although clouds don’t move that fast.... Was there a fire? we were all puzzled for a few minutes.... It turned out to be a steam train speeding along a track below! We drove on and soon were going through a labyrinth of mountain valleys.

On the day of the climb the kids were not as enthusiastic as I was. A five-year wait must have drained it out of them, but I was more excited than ever. After some exertion climbing up the nearest and steepest off track rocky wall and some drama with my daughters phone, all taking place just next to the hostel car park, the kid's decided they wanted to go back to the room. I took them back and made sure they had refreshments and snacks. Of course, the Wi-Fi must have been what swung it for them. Playing on electrical gadgets is way better than taking exercise with your Mum up a mountain. It was just me going up the mountain then!

As I had chosen the safest and easiest path with the kids in mind, I remained confident all would be fine, and it was! The views were stunning, and I felt elated the whole time, with each step there was something new to discover, there were ruins of the old shelters where workers of the mine had once stayed, lakes and beautiful waterfalls.

As I carried on higher and higher the temperature got hotter and hotter. I had to take my coat off. The sun was shining, and the sky was brilliant blue. Later I found out that on this particular day, of all the UK, the hottest weather was in Wales and it reached around 22 degrees! Pretty surreal, but it was just as I had imagined it to be, like a summer's day.

When I got back to the hostel room, I was buzzing and had lots of photos to show the kids. I discovered that they hadn't been able to work out how to connect to the Wi-Fi but found making camps in the shower and hammocks on the bunkbeds, was rather fun instead!

My nephew felt bad that he had missed out on the mountain climb.

I loved that he was inspired by my experience and although I was physically exhausted, I agreed after a little rest to take him up, so, my nephew and I headed back out to the mountain. The girls were happy to stay where they were.

We made it up as far as the big lake and the miner's ruins. I was very impressed with my nephew, how easily he climbed and how far he could throw rocks out across the lake. He could be an Olympic athlete in the making I am sure.

I had the time of my life climbing the Mountain. I felt accomplished and experienced a profound sense of spiritual connection. Although other members of the extended family had wanted to share the mountain experience with me, none of them did, except my nephew on the second hike.

My daughters Dad had tragically passed away from suicide whilst she was just six years old. This had a massive and long-lasting impact on us all. My Mum had suffered for many years with fibromyalgia before it was discovered she had cancer. By the time we were aware of the cancer it was inoperable because it had spread throughout her entire body! Mum died in November 2016.

It was shortly after Mum's death that I shut down emotionally, I felt I had nothing to give and decided to split up with my boyfriend, rather than put him through everything I was dealing with. I also made up my mind that he couldn't give my Daughter and I the support we needed, but never had a discussion to find out if he thought otherwise. I didn't know how to communicate what I was feeling, or thinking, buried underneath it all though I still loved him.

Even though none of these people were physically there on the

mountain, I felt close to everyone I loved up there and felt I was doing it for all of us. Just this thought fills my heart with joy every time, which is exactly what I had wanted.

Going up the mountain was like a key turning which opened up my heart, releasing me from a lonely prison I had created. I began to see clearly that I had pushed people away all my life to protect myself because I was hurt at very young age. All I really wanted was love, and at the times my daughter and I most needed love and even when it was offered to us, I didn't accept it fully, I couldn't believe it was true.

I built a wall around my heart and no one got through that wall. I was punishing myself, being unkind to myself, and not loving myself. It was a big lesson and one I had to take responsibility for because it not only affected me, but my daughter too. This is what I learned through the experience with my ex-boyfriend almost coming back. It may have been too late for him to accept me opening my heart to him, and I have had to deal with feelings of regret and guilt, they were the hardest things to let go of. Ultimately though, I've had to truly forgive myself.

Writing this has really given me closure on that. I have learnt my lessons and I am thankful to my ex-boyfriend and his new partner for the opportunity they gave me to learn, and to myself for being open and wise enough to learn, all the while with a heart that loves more fully now than ever before.

I choose to go forward in my life now keeping my heart open, giving love to my Daughter and to myself. I know the risk of loving others fully is well worth it and it is ok, because I will never shut my

heart off to myself ever again, so I will always have love inside of me, and plenty to share.

I also realised on this epic adventure that if I have a dream I love and want to happen, it is ok to do it myself and in doing so it may or may not inspire others too. Either way I have the power to create my own joy.

Maybe if I had gone ahead and made plans all them years ago, my Mum and my daughters Dad would have come along and experienced it for themselves and felt their own joy. Maybe if I had been open with my boyfriend we would have stayed together, and he would have came to Wales with us, but how would I have known to do that if I hadn't been through the pain of regret and guilt?

I can only speculate about the past, and what great lessons I have learned from it. Since deciding to climb Mount Snowdon my life has drastically improved. I feel this was a pivotal moment. It was the beginning of my true healing. I had one of the most transformational years of my life ever in 2019, I graduated in December from my training with Psycademy. I became certified as a Spiritual Practitioner and Karmic Alignment Coach. Currently I am on the Psycademy team of tutors where I am training to guild students. I have new dreams of coaching others to heal their own heart wounds, because now I know that it is possible.

Despite the extraordinary global events that have been taking place in 2020 with the Covid-19 virus, and the struggles it has presented for many people, personally I have been experiencing an amazing time of growth. I feel very empowered by the decisions I make every day, like the one to change direction with work,

ending a five-year mural and art business to focus on my new coaching skills. Even small decisions like taking regular exercise or taking part in online social events during lockdown are bringing me more health and wellbeing.

I knew for a long time that I wanted to make changes, but I felt stuck. What turned things around for me was deciding to take action, I went out into the world, I decided to go places and connect with the energy of things I loved. Saying ‘one day’ will not get you anywhere. You need to put measurable goals in place by setting time scales, making a date, booking a ticket, and putting the work in.

Here are some things I started doing:

I was invited to go along to a parenting course by our social worker, I accepted and completed all the classes because I wanted to improve my skills being a single Mum.

I did a writing course and went to a few book signing events where I met the authors, this was because I wanted to write a book.

I went to an event put on by Psycademy because I wanted to learn more about how I could help myself and others.

In addition to this I attended a self-love event run by Lisa King, the mastermind and one of the co-creators and authors of this book.

I started doing intuitive artwork that I felt inspired to do rather than take on commissions. I love being creative and making art, but I decided to make art with the purpose of assisting transformation

and healing which I find much more fulfilling. I stopped waiting for things to somehow just magically show up, I went out and found things to do with what I love.

More opportunities have shown up, and now I act upon them quickly, for example by being part of creating this book. If I ever want to do something now but feel hesitant about it, I recognise that it will be either because I have some stuff I need to learn and some resources I need to access, or I will know if it is because I don't feel it in my heart. I feel into my heart to find the answers, is this something I feel love and passion for? If the answer is yes, then I figure out what I need to do. These resources may be hidden deep down, or there may be some steps I need to take or work towards first.

I know I can learn anything I want to, or I can call upon my courage, strength, persistence or whatever is needed. I either look within myself or seek help from someone who has more knowledge or experience than I currently do.

Living a life we love is actually about integrating the mind and the heart, building up openness, trust and communication between them. Taking action is vital and making time scaled plans is too. Above all it is most important that we fill ourselves and our lives up with Love.

We CAN do anything we CHOOSE to do when we do it with love.

We have free will to decide ....you could choose to be miserable and close off to life, letting fear of being hurt and living from the past cloud your vision of the present.

In the worse case choosing to let fear win could mean your dreams end up unlived, leaving them for someone else to fulfil as I did for my Mum and my Daughter's Dad alternatively.

You can choose to follow your heart and live the life you love.

Author: Jodie Lee Liggett

A quirky fact about me: I painted the 'Welcome' mural in the 'Starlight' children's ward at West Middlesex Hospital.

What I do now: Jodie is a spiritual artist and coach. She designs creative interactive tools and energy artwork that are used in. healing processes such as mindfulness, meditation and journaling.

She is a qualified Spiritual Practitioner, Karmic Alignment Coach and a Tutor in training with Psycademy, Leaders in Human Transformation, Healing and Evolution. She delivers coaching to assist people to find their blocks, and Unconscious Programming, often relating to trauma or passed negative experiences.

Not only does she assist people to identify the root cause of their biggest problems but also guides them through a powerful and lasting emotional process called CET, Conscious Emotional Transformation.

How to connect with me:

www.facebook.com/inspiritcreate

@Inspirit_create

I have a message just for you!
Scan me with your camera or QR app

Living A Lie

Lara Costa

"You're gonna realize that it feels so much better to have one person really know you and love you, than to have a hundred people love you and never really know you."

Shannon Beveridge

Do you ever feel like you're living a lie?

If you were with me in early 2018 that would be exactly how you were feeling. You would have found me in my surgery, bright orange scrubs, typing away on a computer. The room was quite small and with no windows. It felt like you were working in a bunker. There was a dental chair right in the middle of the room and it smelled exactly how you would expect a dentist's surgery to smell.

Suddenly, the door bursts open. "How are you my friend?" "I'm very well, I feel amazing today! Thank you for asking. How are you Sophie?" Sophie is this very tall lady with short black hair and a thick Polish accent. She almost gave my dental nurse a heart attack when she burst in through the door. "I have something I need to talk to you about. There's this event in London and I really want to go. It's a personal development thing. I've got a spare ticket. Would you like to come with me?" "Sure, why not? Send me some information so I know where I'm going". Later that evening I was sitting at my desk in the living room. I was renting a flat in a very old Victorian house, so the living room was spacious

with tall ceilings. I decorated it teal, my favourite colour. Then Alex comes in. They are tall, broad shoulders, dark sunken eyes like they haven't slept for days. They greet me with their usual frown and raspy, abrupt manner. "What the hell do you think you're doing?" "Well Alex, Sophie wants to go to this event. It's all around personal development. I'm going with her, I think it will be good for me". "Good? Good for what? Waste of money! Like you are ever going to change, like it will make a difference. You do this over and over again and you're still in the same place. Same shit, different day Lara".

Have you ever felt like this? Like you just don't fit in?

To everyone else, I looked successful. I was always smiling, pretending everything was fine and that life was good. Then, as soon as the door would shut behind me at home, everything changed and I was a completely different person.

Depression manifests differently in each and every one of us. For me, it caused complete inertia. I would go to bed on Friday night and sleep all the way through until Monday morning. The only reason I would get up Monday morning was because I had to go to work. No food, no form of personal hygiene for two days. I just wanted to shut everything out. I had the habit of bottling everything up and never talking about how I felt. Just carrying on, doing the same things every day. I was alive but not living. I felt like I was on the same journey, the same place, same time. I was living in a vicious cycle that was going on and on, this wasn't how I wanted my life to be. It got so bad that I was taking medication and it wasn't making much difference. Anxiety caused me to overthink everything, even the most insignificant things. At this point I was so fed up with everything that I didn't want to carry on. I had written a

suicide letter and planned where I was going to end my life. Nobody had a clue how bad things had gotten.

Despite Alex's reaction, I ended up going with Sophie to that event and decided to sign up for a public speaking course. That's where you would have found me in March 2019, in the foyer of a huge hotel. The foyer was all made of white marble and the room where the event was being held had way too many chairs for my liking. My brain went straight into flight mode. "Well then, now I just need to get myself a chair at the back of the room and near the door. You never know when a zombie apocalypse is going to happen. Why? Why do I keep doing this to myself? Why do I keep putting myself in these situations? I clearly don't belong here!"

This had been my life up until this point. I'd been living a lie. I had a secret, a burden I'd been carrying around for 26 years. This was the day I met Lisa. Lisa was one of the mentors of the course. She has short hair, glasses, wears funky shirts and always has a smile on her face. She was talking to a group of people who were attending the course when I walked in.

I overheard her telling a story about her wife. What got me was how she spoke about her so openly and easily. I couldn't believe she used the word "wife" instead of "partner". I had this incredibly visceral reaction, started shaking and got visibly upset. Lisa noticed that and came over to speak to me.

"Hey, Lara, are you ok? Is there anything you want to talk to me about?"

"Yes , there is. Lisa, there's this thing about me. It's something I have never talked about before. Something that no one knows. It's like a weight on my shoulders. I'm not sure how to talk about it".

"Ok, can I ask you a personal question?" Lisa replied.
Yes, of course you can".

"Is this about your sexuality?"

"Yes. Yes, it is. I'm bisexual and I don't know how to deal with this, I've known for a long time. I'm so scared, it's the first time I have said these words out loud". When those words came out of my mouth, my emotions went into overdrive.

"It's going to be ok, just let your emotions out, you've held them in long enough".

After speaking to Lisa, I felt like a huge weight had been lifted off my shoulders. I'd been holding on to that secret for so long that at times I thought I couldn't go on. I couldn't see the light at the end of the tunnel. I know that if I hadn't met her that day and talked about what was going on in my head, I wouldn't be here to fight another day.

You see, I have always been the person who was cheerful and happy. The one that always had a smile on her face. I was, by societies' standards, successful. I was financially stable, had family and friends who loved me. No one would ever guess that deep down I felt completely worthless and that I was suffering from severe depression and anxiety. I was so deep in the closet that at that point I had found Narnia. However, no epic adventure followed. This meant that every day my emotions were unpredictable, but one thing I did know. I knew I didn't want to live my life like this. Something had to change and that day it did!

Have you ever felt like one moment, one conversation saved your life?

Being able to open up to Lisa and talking things through was my moment, my ticket out of jail. Unfortunately, the road still had some obstacles I needed to overcome. The constant questions I kept asking myself were:

Will I ever be able to come out?
Should I do it?
Am I ready?
Is this the right time?
Is this the right thing to do?
Maybe if I can keep on ignoring my truth, just keep pushing it all down, I will be fine?

After that day I had to go back to reality and at that point reality really sucked for me. Despite this, I was so excited when I got home. I couldn't wait to tell Alex what had happened!

"Alex, I've made a decision! I'm going home and I'm going to tell my family and friends about being bisexual. I know it will be a shock for them, but I'm going to do it". "You're going to tell them? That's hilarious! There's no way that's going to happen. You'll never be able to do it. You're going to do what you always do, you'll avoid it. You're that useless".

Alex was right. I went home and chickened out. I couldn't tell anyone. I felt angry, frustrated, disappointed in myself. Why couldn't I do it? I've achieved so much in my life, far more difficult things. So why couldn't I say 3 simple words?

I needed to do this, I needed to stop living a lie. I had to give myself the chance to be happy, to be me. I had stayed in touch with Lisa and she was giving me the confidence and the belief I needed. One step at a time, you can do this, were the words she would tell me, and that's exactly what I did, I took the first step. I

told a close friend first. I was shaking and cried through the whole conversation, but what matters is I did it.

"Michelle, I have got something I need to speak to you about"
"What is it?"
"It's about me, my sexuality. I'm bisexual"
"Damn, it only took you 26 years to realise that!

I was baffled! She wasn't shocked! She had known for a while but wanted me to feel comfortable enough to speak to her about it. I couldn't believe it! I thought people had no idea!

I continued telling people I trusted, one at a time. Each time I blurted it out it just became easier and easier. Then I came out to my parents, brother and closest family and other friends. My parents were my biggest challenge. They are my rock and have been so supportive of me that I didn't want to disappoint them. I was expecting the conversation to be awful. I ran all the possible scenarios in my head and the outcome was always very dramatic.

Mum and dad were absolutely amazing. They were as they are and have been, loving and supportive and I know they will stand by me no matter what. I was absolutely petrified of what people would think, of my family and friends never talking to me again but the response I got was overwhelmingly positive.

Fast forward a few months and you wouldn't recognise the person that walked into that hotel. I found my voice. This enabled me to open up and start living as my true self.

Since then I've created amazing relationships, joined LGBTQIA+ groups, allowed myself to experience new emotions. I feel like the real Lara blossomed, that weight I was carrying around is no more.

To be honest, there are challenges that still come up from time to time. Biphobia is a real problem and there is a severe stigma in society, even amongst the LGBTQIA+ community. I've lost count of how many times I was told I didn't belong, that I was just curious or that I was undatable because I would definitely dump someone for a person of the opposite sex. The heterosexual community also gives me grief, telling me that I'm just confused, it's just a phase and I'll grow out of it. Now I'm in a position of power that enables me to shut all this down and live my best life. Not as 50% straight and 50% gay, but as a 100% bisexual.

You see, Alex never really left my side when I went back home. They are that voice in your head that's always ready to tell you that you can't do it, that you're not good enough, that you're going to fail. I know that they will always be with me, however now I know how to tame them. It's not always a fight I win, but I now possess the tools to give them a good run for their money.

What strategies do I use, you might wonder? I changed the way I word the situation inside my head. Adjusting the language I use, turning the negatives into positives, made a massive difference in the way I deal with challenges. Now, I ask myself the right questions. Instead of why this or why that, I start with how. How can I change this, how can I improve that? I also avoid self-blaming or ruminating on things and instead ask myself what can I learn from this particular scenario.

However, the most considerable transformation happened when I stopped caring about what other people thought of me. Of course, there is a handful of people whose opinion matters to me. I'm only human. Other than those selected few, if you like me, you like me. If you don't, you don't.

I lost count of the amount of times I heard it gets better. I'm a

sceptical person by nature, so I never believed it. I want you to know that it does. It truly does. You just need to keep on fighting.

You don't have to achieve huge goals every day. I know sometimes you can't, it feels like too much. Getting out of bed, brushing your teeth or having a shower will be a victory and a step forward some days.

Since I came out, I am free. I feel happy and strong. Now, getting up in the morning is exciting and I can't wait to see what the day will bring. There are still some challenging moments but that's part of being alive. Everyone decides to come out at different stages in life and each and every one of our stories is different and that's the beauty of it.

I only want to give you a little piece of advice: the first time you come out make sure the person you're speaking to is understanding and will be supportive of you. I'm aware this isn't always possible in the "real" world, but that's what online communities are for.

I've now stopped living a lie and I'm all me. I just needed to realise that those who mind don't matter and those who matter don't mind.

Author: Lara Costa

A quirky fact about me: I can recite the lines from Harry Potter films word for word.

What I do now: Lara wanted to be a part of this project to empower people in the same situation that she was in, to inspire them and show them that there is hope and that things will get better.

Lara is a qualified dentist and published author. She is also the founder of the Fearless Faculty, a safe space where young LGBTQIA+ can come to connect, meet new people and empower themselves. Lara is passionate about volunteering and helping people live their truth.

Lara loves learning new things, particularly around health. She also loves reading, in particular fantasy novels, science fiction and has a love for Harry Potter.

How to connect with me:

www.facebook.com/thefearlessfaculty

@thefearlessfaculty

@lamlaracosta

I have a message just for you!
Scan me with your camera or QR app

"It's ok for her..." they said.

Leila Singh

How many times have you said, "But it's ok for them…"?

If it were easy, we would all be living our 'ideal life, right? Today, I can say that I am a TEDx Speaker, Founder and Director of my Personal Brand & Coaching Consultancy, an accredited Master Coach and Trainer, Professional Speaker Mentor, NLP Master Practitioner, and an award-winning author.

I have often had people say to me, "well it's ok for you…." Or "you are so lucky…". Yet here is the thing. I am no-one special. I am not especially well-connected, nor was I born with a silver spoon.

I believe that I have had a blessed life, yes, however that is merely my own perspective. And a large part of that perspective is driven by the way I choose to look at things, you could say, my 'rose-tinted lens'. But I will let you decide if that is true.

Let me take you back to when I was a child, around the age of eleven. You would regularly find me perched on my double bed, in my beautifully decorated pink bedroom, pink and white wallpaper, pink and white carpet, and white wardrobes with a hint of pink. The wallpaper, carpet and wardrobes all had a light hint of grey flowing through it. There was a light oak coloured wooden desk and chair to one side, and a dressing table scattered with my toiletries and hair decorations.

My parents were always loving, supportive and encouraging of me

and all that I did. My mum was my best friend. And as I perched on the end of my bed, looking into the mirror, I would be crying, almost daily, wondering why I was the ugly duckling, what had I done to deserve this, thinking how life was so unfair, that no boy would ever fancy me, and why wouldn't it just go away.

This continued well into my early twenties. Ok, perhaps I didn't sit and cry on a daily basis, but the inner dialogue was certainly there, you know, the one that tells you that you are not good enough, pretty enough, smart enough, that passes critical judgement on all that you are, or are not. The result of this? Through my formative years, I was extremely timid, the quiet, shy church mouse, who lacked confidence, had zero self-esteem, and no great belief in my abilities. This continued as I went onto university and subsequently embarked on my dream career journey as an accountant.

This self-judgement influenced many of my decisions. I chose to often hide away, I would decline social invitations, to go for a drink, to a club or party, for fear of what others would say. Although I was heavily into eighties music, I would never dream of attending a music concert. I would avoid trying new things or attending social situations where I would be seen.

Instead, I chose to 'hide', keep my head down, study hard, and aim for good results in my exams. Why? Because I believed that people will never like me for my beauty, so perhaps they will like me for my brains! You might be thinking, 'What was so unfair?' 'What could possibly be going on to have me feeling so inadequate, so inferior to others?' when it was apparent that I experienced a loving, stable and secure upbringing.

Here is the thing; I experienced severe, and I mean severe acne, for almost 17 years. Yes, you heard that right. Not simply a couple

of years as a teenager like most kids, but from the age of 11 through to 27 years old. Whilst I was fortunate to not have been bullied in a big way about my predicament, I did receive the occasional hurtful comment on the condition of my skin.

And so there I was, the good student, good grades, academically smart, (don't get me wrong, I wasn't one of those naturally talented kids, I had to work really hard to get those grades!), graduated from University and went on to qualify as an Accountant. The trouble was, a successful academic track record was not enough when my inner thoughts still had me feeling 'not good enough'.

What needs to happen, for you to take action, to create change in your life?

During the couple of years where I was studying for my professional qualification, still living with my parents, you would have seen me in my bedroom, and yes, it was still pink, white and grey, in May of 1997, sat at my desk, studying diligently late into the night, when all of a sudden, "Mummy, Mummy, I can't see, I can't see, I've gone blind! Mummy, please help me". My mum, bleary-eyed from being woken from her sleep, opened my bedroom door as she rushed over to where I was sat at my desk.
"Mummy I can't see, my vision has gone! Everything is dark! What's happening? Mummy, I'm scared". "Leila, it's two in the morning, you are tired, let's get you into bed, and get some rest, and we will decide what to do in the morning..." My mum helped me to bed, and I promptly fell asleep.

As my radio alarm came on the next morning and awoke me, the memory of the night before came flooding back. I slowly opened one eye, feeling nervous, and looked around. It was still dark in the room, but I could just see the light peeping through the gap at the top of the curtains. I then opened my other eye and did the same,

and again could see the light peeping through. As I sighed with relief and opened both eyes, my mum came dashing in to see how I was doing. "I know it's those stupid pills I have been taking! The doctor keeps saying they are fine to take, but they aren't solving the problem, they are like a plaster, a temporary fix. I have been taking those pills like smarties whilst I have been revising! And yet I still keep getting daily migraines!"

"Leila, you are under a lot of pressure, what with your job and the long hours coupled with your studies. Perhaps you need to get more rest..." "No mum, I know it's this cocktail of drugs. The ones he prescribed for my skin clearly states 'do not take if you suffer from headaches or migraines' and yet he says it's all good. Then he prescribes the ones for the migraines, it's all too much! And they are not even working! Enough is enough! I will find another way!"

What compelled me to pick up a copy of the 'Yellow Pages' (a paper version of what we now know as Google!), I cannot say. I did not know what I was looking for, yet my eyes fell upon a section that had the phone numbers of Reflexologists. I didn't even know what one was, but I picked out a number and rang it.

The lovely lady on the end of the phone took the time to explain to me how the treatment worked, and I promptly booked my first appointment with her. In case you are wondering, this was pure instinct on my part, nothing else. After the first couple of treatments my migraines began to subside, until, within a few weeks, I had them under control. Over 20 years later and I still receive reflexology for maintenance of my health. Upon reflection, since then, subconsciously, I have always found myself naturally searching for holistic solutions to any health challenges I experience.

The lovely lady persuaded me over the first few months to consider food testing, to address my acne (still severe at this time). I resisted for months, as I felt that, based on the sacrifices I would have to make, I was not prepared to do so, just yet.

Eventually, when I had a break between jobs, I decided to have the food testing done and whilst feeling as though I would haemorrhage during the first 12 days, (of my body detoxing), within a matter of months, my skin cleared up, I felt comfortable to face the world without caking on make-up! My overall health and energy soared, and I felt truly amazing! This was not an easy process; it required discipline, commitment, and sacrifice. Yet the results were fantastic and more than I could have wished for!

"Have you ever wanted to experience a big change in any aspect of your life, and what were you prepared to do differently or to sacrifice, to create that change?"

So, what was the consequence of this? Following my gut instinct, changing my eating habits for good, continuing my reflexology treatments, and quitting listening to our Doctor, (who was subsequently struck off in part for his ineptitude) changed my life! Simply feeling better in myself, improved health, energy, and clarity, creating an element of confidence, my self-esteem began to develop, and my inner dialogue began to shift.

I continued to pursue my dream career in accountancy, had a great job that I enjoyed, in a global Telco organisation. During that time, the guy that had hired me, John, came by my desk to say goodbye, as he was moving onto pastures new.

"Leila, you have been a great hire for the team and the organisation, you over-deliver, meet your deadlines and we are pleased with your performance. When I think about your career

aspirations that you shared with me during your interview, I have no doubt that you have the capabilities to achieve these, yet my feeling is that you will struggle. Why? Because people don't know who you are, your strengths, the great work that you do, other than myself and your team leader. My advice to you is this, you need to make yourself known, to those that matter, sing your own praises for the work that you do, and speak up more, voice your opinions and ideas…" What John said made sense, yet I really did not know what to do.

As my confidence grew, I began to speak up a little, I applied for a technical finance role, something that I hadn't done before. I remember being worried about whether I would have the ability to carry out the role well. Speaking with a work friend about this, she said something that I always carry with me, *"Leila, you can achieve anything you put your mind to!"* She was right.

The role was challenging, yet I excelled in it, and as time went by, I began to realise that I wanted more. Something was missing and I could not quite place what it was. I began a journey of self-reflection, exploring aspects of the various roles I had been exposed to, what I really enjoyed, what energised me, and what drained me.

One morning in mid-November 2000, you would have seen me walking towards our 'goldfish bowl' meeting room, a large glass meeting room in the middle of our open-plan office, with a large white oval boardroom style table in the middle. Peter, late 30's, about 5'10", wavy blonde hair and blue eyes, a super-smart Cambridge graduate, walked alongside me. "How was your weekend Leila?" "Oh, it was lovely, caught up with friends, relaxed a little, yourself?" "Far too short…" as he held open the glass door for me to enter. "What is that you have there, Leila, certainly not what it looks like…." As I slid the white envelope across the table,

there was a long pause, then a sigh... "I don't understand, I thought you were happy here, you enjoyed working in our team...is it the money? I can look into that, we can accelerate the plan we have in place for you, for the team leader role! Really, Leila, I don't want you to leave!" "Peter, it isn't the money, I am taking a huge pay-cut, and yes, I have thought this through, at length. You are right, I am happy here, I love working in our team, and for you, it's just...I want something more. It has taken me a while to figure it out, and I have done my research, my due diligence..."

"Pay cut? What do you mean? You are about to complete on your new home, how can you possibly afford to take a pay-cut when you are already stretching yourself?" "It's a 50% pay-cut, Peter, and it's ok, really, it sounds crazy, but I know it will work out just fine. It's a sales role, I am going to be a recruitment consultant...." "50%... Recruitment... You are throwing away everything you have worked for! I really think you need to reconsider this. I will leave it open to you for a while. Let me know what you decide..."

As it happened, the following week, November 20th, I was due to complete on my first home, I had it all planned. I had booked the afternoon off work, to collect my keys, and my mum would join me to go to my new home, I was very excited!

On Saturday 18th November, I dropped my mum to her friend's home for lunch and popped to the mall to grab some last-minute things for my new home. I received a call from her friend within an hour. "Your mum collapsed on the stairs, and couldn't move her legs, we called an ambulance. She is on her way to the hospital."
My mum, a fiercely strong and independent lady, had taken early retirement from her job just months earlier when she turned 60. She had plans to travel and do all the things that she had not been able to do whilst she was bringing up a family and working.

Monday 20th arrived, and we were none the wiser. I had gone to work as normal, only to break down crying when Peter asked how my weekend had been. He sent me home and told me to do whatever I needed to do. I spent the rest of the day at the hospital, apart from a quick dash to the estate agents to collect my keys. The consultant, a tall slim young man with short dark hair, chocolate brown skin, and black-rimmed glasses perched on the end of his nose, summoned my Dad and me to the hospital that evening for 11pm.

As we stood outside the room that my mum was lying in, he began, "Mr Singh, Layla (as I am often mistakenly called), I am sorry to call you in so late in the evening. After numerous tests and scans, we have discovered that Mrs Singh has a tumour growing against her spine. Her fall was a consequence of the tumour, finally damaging her spine. I am afraid she will never walk again. Tests show that she has multiple myeloma, a bone marrow cancer…"

The rest of what he said was a blur. The tragic news, the shock, the massive impact on all of us, was too much to take in.

What would you have done had you found yourself in this situation?

Of course, I had choices. I could have rescinded my resignation and remained comfortable in my finance role. I didn't. I did defer moving out of home, as following my mum's return home three months later, I was her primary carer initially, with my dad taking some months to get his head around what had happened. I embarked on my new career in recruitment in January 2001, having deferred my start date by a few weeks.

2001 was a challenging year. The gradual acceptance of my

mum's situation, being her primary carer for the greater part of that year, and in a new job that stretched me so far out my comfort zone that it hurt! Yet at my performance review a year into the role, my Director acknowledged that whilst they had taken a risk on me, with no sales experience, they were exceptionally pleased that I had achieved the status of highest biller in my first year, amongst a team of seasoned Consultants. I remembered this… *"Leila, you can achieve anything you put your mind to!"*

My biggest learnings during that time were, that no-one is better than me, my inferiority complex had been overcome, and we are all equal, with our own value to bring to the world. And some people value my views, opinions, and ideas, so long as I speak up and share them!

Upon reflection, I realised that almost subconsciously I had taken on board John's comments, to show up and speak up! And by taking on a role that took me so far out my comfort zone, I realised what I was truly capable of! I earned more in that first year than I would have done, had I stayed in my finance role.

What really hit home for me was this; if I don't step out my comfort zone, take risks, try new things, and do the things I really want to do, the only person missing out is me. No one else cares. It was during this time that I quickly realised that it was time to let go of incessant self-judgment and criticism of myself, as well as others' opinions, and embrace what life had to offer.

My mum's predicament taught me how valuable life is, and how important it is to grab opportunities and make the most of what we have, in the here and now. She never got to fulfil all her dreams, the travel she had planned. And whilst the consultant's prognosis for my mum was two years, I am forever grateful that my mum was with us for another 13 years. And for the most part, she was

always smiling, never complained, and remained independent as far as was possible. Her determination saw no bounds. This taught me the strength of mind, appreciation for what we have, and reduced my tolerance for people with their inane dramas and complaints of things they can change.

Why do we have to experience such trauma and tragedy, to learn these lessons in life?

What happened next?

A couple of years on, following redundancy, I accepted a role at what is now Hewlett Packard Enterprise (HPE) (formerly Electronic Data Systems). Corporate Finance and Treasury Consultant. A role I had virtually no experience of, yet I was determined to secure the position. Had I been put forward for that role two or more years earlier, I believe that I would not have even been considered for an interview.

I excelled in a role where I learnt from the ground up, gained new skills and experiences I would never have dreamt of, as I continued to evolve and grow. I enjoyed a range of corporate hospitality events with our financiers and lenders, perhaps the most enjoyable six years of my career! When HPE acquired EDS in 2008, I was offered two opportunities. I accepted the Treasury Consulting role, as it was very different from what I knew and provided another perspective of Treasury.

Fifteen months later, I accepted the previous opportunity, as a Sales Executive. Almost ten years in the role, I delivered a little shy of $1bn of business, received several awards for my sales performance, asked for and received a 17% pay-rise, and developed long-lasting and valuable professional relationships.

Notice a pattern here; For most of my career, I have had very limited experience of the roles I have taken on. Each time I have taken risks, tried new things, stepped out my comfort zone and yet still achieved success!

In 2013, after my mum passed, and in parallel to my Sales role at HPE, I began to immerse myself further in my personal growth journey. I invested time, energy, and money in surrounding myself with the best coaches and mentors! I trained and qualified as a Master Practitioner in Neuro-Linguistic Programming. It was during this time that I realised the potential of the mind, and moreover that we are all capable of so much more than we realise. This is when I truly accepted that yes, I can achieve anything I put my mind to!

Over 3 months, I wrote and published my award-winning book, "Success Redefined – How to Leverage Your Natural Talents to be Limitless" in 2015, overcame my fear of public speaking and became an accredited Professional Speaking mentor for others, I did a board break, walked bare foot across hot coals, and broken glass, qualified as an accredited Master Coach and Coach Trainer, L&D trainer, all alongside my full time and demanding sales role.

The pinnacle of my personal growth journey thus far is the opportunity to become a TEDx Speaker in December 2019. Is this something I ever imagined possible? Not until the last couple of years…and I am not going to lie, I was close to pulling out of this for fear of 'not being good enough' and of other's judgement!

I loved my sales role, my colleagues, and clients, and was earning a six-figure salary. Yet, in December 2018 I finally chose to leave my corporate career. Why? Because I wanted something more. I wanted to follow my passion, to enable others to take risks, step up and be visible, realise that they can achieve anything they put their mind to, that anything is possible. And that it all starts with you.

So when you look at me and think, “it's ok for her…” remember, we all have our own journey, challenges, choices in what we do, how we choose to perceive the world around us, and what we want our reality to be. I chose to work on showing up as the best version of me, in all that I do, and in turn to serve and inspire others to be the best version of themselves!

When I reflect upon my accomplishments over the years, I would never have believed my life would turn out this way. And for this, I am proud, humbled, and excited for what lies ahead!

And my only wish is that through sharing my journey, I may inspire at least one person to take action, to create the change they desire, and to live the best version of themselves!

What steps are you not taking, for fear of not being good enough?

What opportunities are you missing out on, for fear of what others might say?

And how will you realise what you are truly capable of, if you continue to hide within your comfort zone?

Remember this: Change is inevitable, yet uncomfortable. To create the change you desire in your life, you have to be prepared to change within yourself.

I invite you to take some time to reflect on where you are today, where you would like to be, create a plan of baby steps, actions that you can take, starting today! And I wish you all the success in the world!

“Your dreams of today can be your future reality!”

Author: Leila Singh

A quirky fact about me: I am a Tony Hadley groupie –I even flew to Rome to see him perform a Frank Sinatra tribute concert!

What I do now: Leila Singh is an accomplished Sales and Finance professional with a Corporate career spanning over 25 years, and a wealth of experience initially gained as a qualified Accountant (FCCA), Recruitment Consultant, Corporate Finance and Treasury Consultant, and latterly a successful Sales Executive delivering shy of $1bn of business at Hewlett Packard Enterprise where she spent 15 years.

Furthermore, Leila, now a Personal Brand Consultant and TEDx Speaker, is accredited as a Master Coach and Master Coach Trainer, L&D Trainer and Mentor at the Professional Speakers Academy, as well as a Certified Master Practitioner of Neuro Linguistic Programming (NLP) & Hypnotherapy. She is also the Author of the award winning book, "Success Redefined – How to Leverage your Natural Talents to be Limitless!"

As Managing Director of Success Redefined Limited and Founder of mi-brand™, a Personal Brand and Coaching Consultancy, Leila draws her on her wealth and breadth of skills, knowledge and experience in the area of sales, finance and professional growth, to enable her framework, 'The Unique Personal Brand Blueprint™' which has resulted in increased salaries (averaging 47%) and career advancement, through enhancing their visibility, impact, and influence, increasing performance and results, and ultimately standing out as a leader amongst peers, customers, in their teams, organisations and industry.

You can watch Leila's TEDx talk here: https://leilasingh.com/TEDx

How to connect with me:

 www.facebook.com/leilasingh001

 www.instagram.com/leila_singh001/

 www.linkedin.com/in/leila-singh/

 www.twitter.com/leila_singh001

www.leila-singh.mykajabi.com/personal-brand-launchpad

I have a message just for you!
Scan me with your camera or QR app

"Mummy, You Don't Love Me"

Christina (Tina) Valentine

Unravelling the true meaning of Daisy's language

I often get asked, 'is she yours?' just because I'm white and I'm gay; like I've somehow acquired this little brown child who's calling me Mummy. Well, Daisy is mine and I am her biological Mum. Why do I feel like I'm not Daisy's Mum sometimes though?

It's almost midnight, April 21st 1997 on a cold wet Thursday night. I'm sat parked up with Daisy in my old Chevrolet Blazer Jeep in Soho Square, Central London. She's been asleep for ages next to me in the passenger seat snuggled up in her little booster seat. Daisy's 4 years old and a pretty smiley face with her brown tight curly hair all tied up tight in a top scrunchy. Daisy looks so very blissful as she sleeps; yet I sit here almost unaware tears are steaming down my face. I cry in silence. I'm not sure how long we've been sat here.

I hope Daisy wakes up soon. I'm so lost in my thoughts though; I make no attempt to rouse her. She was so excited earlier about going to go the Trocadero Arcade to play Bop the Crocs.

I'm so confused. The divide between my conflicting thoughts and feelings is cavernous and I struggle to make sense of anything anymore.

'Am I the bad Mum I'm led to think I am, or is that his portrayal of me that I've come to believe as my own or am I a good Mum and it's him that's bad?'

Nothing is clear anymore.

And sitting here is not helping. I start driving, with the voices ringing in my head the whole time, 'you're a bad Mother. You can't look after Daisy. Daisy doesn't want to be with you.'

Yet somehow, I willingly corroborate with my voices. As we leave London I pull into a petrol station getting myself a carrier bag full of food. As I drive, I greedily stuff down cakes, chocolate and crisps, washing down barley chewed mouthfuls with strawberry milk shake helping get it down my throat faster. Gorging myself perfectly serves the purpose of reinforcing the negative voices, almost making them truly mine. I drive for ages, heading to the coastline with Daisy blissfully unaware she'll not be Bopping the Crocs tonight. The silent tears freely roll down my face, like somehow they're another part of me crying out to be heard.

"What's in the bag Mummy?" Still half sleep, Daisy reaches for the carrier bag and rummages around amongst the empty wrappers finding one last packet of crisps. She happily opens them thinking we're still on our way to the Trocadero. I can see her out of the corner of my eye and watch her cute slightly chubby little hand pull out the crisps one at a time.

"Here you are Mummy, one for you." I try my hardest to stop my tears from falling as I look over and smile back at her taking the crisp. In that moment something shifts in me like a bolt of lightning going through me and I'm no longer trapped in my head hearing the voices 'You're a bad mother'. Instead I feel an overwhelming gut sense screaming 'I am a good Mother and I will protect Daisy no matter what.'

At my mental breaking point, my inner gut cries breakthrough and for the first time ever I hear myself with total clarity and trust and I

know what I need to do.

We share the crisps. I turn around and we go home.

"Dr Graffy, I think I'm depressed. Last night my ongoing confusion between my conflicting thoughts and feelings was at absolute breaking point and I ended up making my way towards to Beachy Head with Daisy to make my final decision.

I could hear my head saying:

- 'You're a bad Mum and him and Julie are wonderful 'parents' to Daisy. Go back home tonight Tina and drop Daisy down to them in the morning. Return alone because Daisy is better off without you.'

Then with far greater intensity my heart and gut instincts would override those thoughts telling me:

- 'You're a good Mum and it is him that is bad.'

But then the terrifying voices would interject making me believe:

- 'If he really is that bad, think what else is he capable of. You'll never be able to protect Daisy from him ever getting his hands on her again unless you go together.'

The closer I got to my destination the more I believed my gut feelings were right about him, but I also believed that I was powerless to stand up to him; so I made my decision that I was going to protect Daisy and do it the only way I could see was possible in that moment.

But then Daisy woke up and that's why I'm here now.

Dr Graffy listened intently and this was the start of being heard and taken seriously for the first time in my life, where I was able to start

talking about my most deep-seated fears about 'him' my Dad and his relationship with my daughter - his granddaughter Daisy. These fears were way deeper than the day-to-day surface problems of his and Julie's over involvement in our lives.

'Mummy, one for you,' taking that crisp was my awakening moment. I felt like a Phoenix rising from the ashes and I no longer felt the terror of what the truth may uncover. Being supported by Dr Graffy was the external validation I desperately needed to hold on to my new beliefs and start taking the steps needed to stand up to my Dad.

No longer did I believe Dad's voices in my head that I had come to believe were mine.

If Daisy hadn't have woken up though, I would have got to Beachy Head and this is would have been our legacy.

National Newspapers 1997
Tragic Double Deaths
Wrecked car found on the beach after mother plunges with her young daughter to their deaths off Beachy Head Cliffs

The fact that I'm alive today to be able to share my story is the reason I am sharing. If it helps even just one person, everything Daisy and I have gone through has been worth the price we have paid.

Where it all begins… July 1991 and I'm 26 years old. I'm wearing my favourite purple nylon shell suit, matching purple suede wallabies, leather bum bag, and my long permed hair is tied up in a top ponytail.

Off I go to Vadims Gay Club. Like many gay clubs, it's hidden out

of sight, down a dark staircase in a dingy basement of a beautiful Victorian building along the triangle of Park Street, Bristol.

There he is blocking the doorway at the top of the staircase – the club's bouncer Vernon. A champion body builder, with a shiny shaven head and a big smile, slightly misaligned sideways jaw and the most beautifully shaped eyebrows, like a woman's plucked them. I might be gay, but he is very pleasing to the eye and has a deep Jamaican accent with a Bristolian twang.

"Hi Vernon, would you help me?"

"What ya want Baby?"

"Actually Vern, that's exactly what I want – a baby. Can you help?"

"Sure ting, and we do it da right way."

Knowing Vernon's a hot-blooded womaniser, I'd already anticipated he wouldn't be up for the turkey baster method! But you know what, when your goal is big enough you'll do what you need to do to achieve that goal!

Thankfully though, just 3 months later by October 1991 I'm pregnant. This is to be Vernon's 7th child he's fathered, by 6 mothers and still counting…

Life and pregnancy is going pretty well. I've got myself a new girlfriend Laura and we're really excited about Daisy coming into the world. Laura's my age 26, a hairdresser and very distinctive looking. She has short-cropped black hair, bright red lipstick and looks like a pierced and tattooed Betty Boop covered from head to toe in beautiful flowers, fairies and waterfalls and numerous piercings.

My growing niggle though is my parents continued intrusion into my life, including Mum flirting with my partner, although this time she's failing miserably. Laura's pretty repulsed by it to be quite frank - a blessing for me for once. Mum's pretty, blonde and petite a cross between Goldie Hawn and Farrah Fawcett Majors. Mum often flirts with my partners, especially the 'butches'. Despite me feeling uncomfortable about it, no else seems to be bothered. In fact, most seem to get great delight from it, including Dad. Dad's not such a catch; more like a big-eared Rolf Harris with a badly fitting toupee that when the wind blows you can still see his baldhead!

Maybe Mum's flirting with women – albeit my women - gives Dad a false sense of security, thinking she won't then get up to her old tricks with other men.

There was a time I was less knowingly bothered by it all…

See, I once had a secret best friend, my saviour from around the age of 15. We used to do things in secret together and I'd feel better for a short while. My friend helped me with my feelings and emotions. Sometimes we'd have to go the public toilets behind Woolworth in Weston- Super-Mare to do our thing when we couldn't get away with doing at home. Not that anybody would have been bothered; I just didn't want to be found out and doing our thing silently was quite a task to master.

I can still vividly remember being in the toilet cubicles that had weird toilet bowls and being ready to explode. The moment of elation was coming… (Retching sounds) projectile vomiting directly into the battered reflective metal toilet bowls, vomit exploding everywhere.

These toilets were pretty gross, but getting away with purging

myself of all my unwanted feelings and emotions served to perversely heighten my elation. Every time though, my elation was short-lived knowing I'd soon be swallowing more of my parents all over again, ready for the next bout.

The problem now though is I'm pregnant, so my 'friend' can't help me now. I won't do to my baby what I do to myself. She will never be silenced.

The day has finally come, 13th June 1992 and Daisy's arrives into the world with Laura at the birth. Daisy's so cute, born with loads of black wavy hair and all stuck to her head. But no sooner Laura and I bring Daisy home to enjoy life together, my own family's intrusion intensifies.

"Teen, let Mom move in with you to help you with the baby. How are you going to manage?"

"Dad, don't worry. I don't need Mum or Julie or you thanks. I'm doing just fine."

I am sick of 'rescuing' Mum always in the guise of it being for my benefit. I've spent years covering for her when she's been seeing men behind Dad's back. At the back of his mind though, he must know. Does Dad really think Mum being here with me will stop her? It wouldn't be the first time she's brought a man to my house and left wet patches in the bed. On one occasion I remember she used the bed in the spare room during the day where Julie was sleeping that night!

Julie is my older sister; she has never been Mum's confidant/best friend/cover story, whatever you want to call it, as I have. But then we've always been different characters. Julie was an insipid child, unlike me, loud and ballsy. Strangely though, Julie has grown into

a double of Vicky Pollard of Little Britain. Unbelievable transformation!

By September 1993, Daisy's 15 months old and I am done with my family's constant intrusion. We're off, not even Laura, just Daisy and me, and off we go to live in London. It's a brilliant shared lesbian household in Stoke Newington, North London. There's two other lesbian Mums, each with a little boy. I shave off all of my hair for a new London lesbian look. Life is fantastic and I feel so free. Daisy and I enjoy the first three months and our very first Christmas together without 'them' Mum, Dad and Julie being all over Daisy, whilst treating me like I'm some kind of surrogate to be eradicated.

Our happiness is very short lived. New Year's Day 1994, Dad arrives on my doorstep distraught and in tears. Mum has finally left him and gone off with her affair - a Rastafarian half her age in Weston. I know him from School. He was in the year below me.

Our freedom is over. Once again I perform like a circus animal, now dancing to Dad's emotional and psychological whip. Over the next few years until just after Daisy's 5th birthday 13th June 1999, both Dad and Julie's inveiglement into our lives and appropriation of Daisy takes on a whole new level. Out of the frying pan of Mum, into the fire of Dad and Julie...yet still in guise it's all for Daisy's benefit and mine and how very appreciative I should be.

After moving to London, I work as a self-employed painter and decorator and Daisy goes to nursery. I often take her to work with me though, as she's ill quite often with various aliments and just wants to be with me. She happily lies inside her sleeping bag on her blow up Barbie mattress, with all her gel pens and paper, drawing and colouring away for hours on end. Daisy's favourite though is to draw on my rolls of lining paper that I lay out with a tin

of paint at each end, until I need them back to hang on customer's walls. My customers are always strangely happy too to have Daisy on site, despite unwittingly having her drawings on the backside of their lined walls! Daisy and I laugh every time.

Other times Dad and Julie take Daisy on Butlins caravan holidays and to Disney Land Paris. Dad and Julie go on many holidays, every time taking Daisy with them, and other people's children too sometimes - a nice thing to do isn't it? I do wonder though if it's because Julie can't have children of her own. She doesn't always hide her resentment and bitterness about other women having kids so easily when she can't.

Everything is so seemingly fun for Daisy, so why am I constantly battling between my conflicting thoughts and feelings. One minute I trust my thoughts and doubt my instincts, and then something triggers me into doubting those thoughts and shifts me into trusting my gut feelings are telling me the truth. The bigger this divide gets, the more I feel like I'm going mad and the less I can make sense of any of it.

I can't see what I'm looking for with my physical eyes, but I sure can sense it.

"Mummy, you don't love me."
"Daisy darling, I do love you. I don't understand why do you think I don't love you?"
"Mummy, you don't love me. Only Grandad loves me."

I don't understand what Daisy is saying to me. The divide between my head and my gut feelings is at breaking point and I need to know which is right.

"Daisy, I do love you. I love you just as much as Grandad does."

"No Mummy. Only Grandad loves me. Grandad gives me big kisses and cuddles."
"I give you big kisses and cuddles too, don't I?"
"No Mummy, only Grandad."

Daisy looks so very sad every time she tells me that I don't love her. No amount of me telling her that I do love her makes any difference at all. She clearly believes that I'm lying. And as Daisy's Mum, I feel sad and confused when she says, 'I want Grandad, only he loves me.'

Am I such a bad Mum that I have left the roles wide open for Dad and Julie - Daisy's Grandad and Aunt - to simply assume parental roles of my daughter, because that's what it looks like?

I feel sick when I hear Daisy call Grandad 'Dad'. "Daisy, Grandad is not your Dad, he's your Grandad. His name is Grandad.". "Oh, she's alright my little lovely jubbly," encouraging Daisy to carry on calling him Dad. I feel sick. I am Daisy's Mum and if he were Daisy's Dad, work it out...it's repulsive.

Life carries on for another couple of years and all the while I'm watching through my 3rd eye, looking for my evidence. It's so hard though because I'm soon pulled back into seeing life through their eyes. It's like being in a play of my own life. One minute I'm in the audience and I get a glimpse of what really going on with all the characters. But all too soon, I'm pulled right back into the play, and can only see what is portrayed to me.

It's February 1997 and we're now living in a shared household that I've set up in Stamford Hill, North London. We're all lesbians apart from Julie who I've given a room to. I'm trying to help her break away from Dad to have a life of her own.

April 21st 1997. “Daisy darling, do you want to go to the Trocodero Arcades? We can play your favourite Bop the Croc.” (This is that night that could have so easily been fatal but thankfully Daisy woke up and I saw Dr Graffy the following day).

Since seeing Dr Graffy, I see the family worker Alice every week to discuss my deepest fears about my Dad. From day one, Alice tells me to keep a daily journal of what’s going on and conversations Daisy and I have about granddad. Much of the conversations don’t make sense although my suspicions about my Dad become increasingly stronger.

Six weeks after starting to see Alice, its Daisy’s 5th birthday party June 13th 1997. It’s a hot summer’s day and her school friends are celebrating with her all playing in the garden on the bouncy castle, ball pond and paddling pool that I‘ve hired especially. Dad and Julie also enjoy the party. Dad in particular – either sitting in a deck chair watching the little girls play in the paddling pool or getting in the ball pond with them.

For a while now, it’s like I’m watching Dad and he’s watching me, both of us keeping score and neither one of us saying anything about the undercurrent; we just carry on playing happy families. After the party Dad and Julie take Daisy off for yet another a caravan holiday for her birthday this time. Throughout Daisy’s birthday party I watched his every move, with every child like an undercover detective. And it didn’t sit right with me what I saw and heard. It’s ringing in my head as loud as when he said it sat in that deck chair, ‘Cor, she’s a pretty little girl int she, that one’ – Abigail, a pretty little 5 year girl in her red polka dot bikini jumping in and out of the paddling pool. Yet, still not enough to me to know for sure.

Upon Daisy’s return from the caravan holiday, Daisy is more

insistent than ever that I don't love her. I have to understand.

Dear Dad,

I need to say something to you. I feel you are too emotionally dependent on Daisy and it is not fair on her, as it is making her very confused about love and who loves her. Daisy and I need some space from you and so I don't want you seeing Daisy for the time being. Daisy and I need time alone together. Please respect what I am saying and do not undermine me as Daisy's parent and what I believe is best for her….

Love Tina

I write this letter in the hope that Dad will respect what I ask of him and give me the space I need to work things out. However, I don't get what I ask for, but I do get what I need from him - Dad reveals his true colours, instantly attacking me, telling me I'm sick in the head and as twisted as Mum. He doesn't realise but his actions help me put to rest any last hopes that I secretly clung to that perhaps I am wrong about him.

"Julie, look at how Dad is treating me since my letter to him, I need your help to protect Daisy." Naïvely I believe she'll understand and support me. It's many more years though before I find out the truth about Julie. But him, Dad, he instantly reveals what's behind the disguise, going from being the jovial toupeed Rolf Harris into the frightening Kiddie Catcher on Chitty Chitty Bang Bang.

Over the next few months I receive numerous threatening and abusive letters and phone calls, harassment and stalking from 'him'…I struggle to say the name Dad anymore.

Daisy is scared and has nightmares and sleeps in my bedroom on a little mattress at the end of my bed tightly squashed into a corner to feel safe. The bedroom is in the attic room on the 3rd floor. I lock us in every night with the high security lock I have fitted into the thick fire door so he can't get and abduct her in the night. Julie's told me that he's re-mortgaged his house and plans on snatching Daisy and leaving the country with her.

It's now been 3 months that Daisy has not seen Grandad and she's slowly revealing more stuff. It's the 13th August 1997. Daisy is awake at 6am and is drawing a picture lying on the carpet besides my bed.

"Mummy, do you like my picture?"

Still half asleep, I look down and I'm shocked at what I see. Daisy is excellent at drawing but how does she even know about what she's drawing?

"Darling, that's really good," I do my best to answer in my usual voice trying desperately hard not to show my distress at what I see, "why don't you finish it for me while I snooze a bit longer." Seemingly reassured that I am not cross or displeased with her and what she's drawing, Daisy continues to draw.

The drawing is detailed. Grandad is in the picture. Daisy always draws Grandad with his big sticking out ears looking like wing nuts. He's naked. He has a big penis. The balls are big and saggy with stuff squirting out of the end of his penis. Daisy is in the picture. She is smiling. There are bags of sweets in the picture and it appears they are having fun. Grandad is smiling.

Daisy's drawing is unequivocal and I now understand what Daisy has been saying all along.

This one drawing is the start of the uncovering of the true meaning of Daisy's language and in this moment life changes forever.

All this time I have been hearing 'his' words 'Mummy, doesn't love you. Only Grandad loves you', coming out of Daisy's mouth as 'Mummy, you don't love me, only Grandad loves me'. Daisy is right and always has been. I don't 'love' her like Grandad does and nor will I ever.

This is the secret language used by my paedophile Dad, Daisy's Grandad when grooming her into believing that his sexual abuse and exploitation of her is 'love' - their special 'love' that only people who love children do.

Despite being able to speak, he has silenced Daisy from infancy to 5 years old, her most formative years with a language I couldn't understand until now. He has underestimated Daisy and I. She now has a voice and he will never silence her or me again.

Over the following weeks and months Daisy discloses in greater detail everything that has happened. My daily journal of the unfolding disclosure starts to make more sense as the pieces of the puzzle are put together. After 6 months of journaling the picture is crystal clear and suddenly everything makes sense with such clarity.

Discovering my own Dad had been sexually abusing Daisy for as long as she could remember was devastating beyond words. Coming to terms with his ultimate betrayal of my trust, his grooming, exploitation and sexual abuse of my child, living with the reoccurring images in my mind of what he's done, single handily taking on The System to stop him ever getting his hands on Daisy again, whilst also supporting and counselling Daisy through her trauma; required strength, determination and an unshakeable

belief in myself that I didn't know I had in me until I was put to the test.

I am not saying for a minute it was easy. It was a daily battle for many years. Standing up to my Dad when I wrote that letter was the start of me standing up to anyone and everyone whenever I needed to; starting with my Mum, Julie, my brother Paul who all sided with Dad, The Legal System that failed us, Social Services who blamed me, Child Mental Health Services that failed to help when Daisy was self harming, the School that failed to help Daisy when she was being severely bullied by pupils and her male teacher, Julie when she abducted Daisy on her 11th birthday, Adult Mental Health Services when Daisy's 20 and suicidal to name but a few.

All of this has been hard. The hardest step of all though was that very first step of standing up to Dad - something no daughter should ever have to do. After that, every other challenge became just another step, with each one getting less difficult because I grew stronger with every step.

For Daisy's it was the start of a very long, painful and confusing emotional roller coaster journey, firstly having to come to terms with losing Grandad, who she at that time 'believed' was the only person who loved her and then I took him away from her.

To the 5-year-old Daisy, all of this was far beyond her cognitive development to be able to process and make sense of it all. Daisy wanted to protect him and take the blame herself because Grandad told her he was sad and would kill himself if she didn't love him and make him happy. The ripple effect of the extensive psychological grooming and sexual abuse at the hands of Grandad and collusive aunt Julie are still with Daisy today. She's just turned 28 and to this day Julie continues to collude with Dad and do his

dirty work, still harassing and stalking Daisy in her warped attempt at drawing Daisy back into the family.

If I hadn't have acted upon what my gut feelings were telling me and taken my first step to standing up to Dad by writing that letter, Daisy would never have had the safe space she needed to be able to slowly disclose; and I believe in the end Dad and Julie would have managed to completely appropriate Daisy, and who knows what would have happened to me.

Despite his expert psychological grooming of me, he never managed to silence my 6th sense. I am so thankful to myself that I was able to trust my feelings, above and beyond the indoctrinated beliefs in my head, that were never mine to be believed. Trusting that you can believe your gut feelings is a very difficult concept to grasp because gut feelings are intangible and as humans we like concrete tangible facts.

If my story resonates with you, perhaps you've been in or are in a similar situation right now – as if it's in the air, but you can't quite put a finger on it. Perhaps you're sensing something that doesn't marry up with the thoughts in your head. It could be anything, not only Child Sexual Abuse and Exploitation. It's any time that you are duped, cheated on, lied to, abused or betrayed; yet deceived, coerced or persuaded to believe otherwise.

Do you ever wonder how much of what you think that wears you, is not yours to be believed and burdened with?

If so, trust your gut feelings, learn to understand them and act upon them. They will serve you well. You may not get what you want but you will get what you need and your life turn out better for it.

Author: Christina (Tina) Valentine

A quirky fact about me: I can still do a one handed hand stand at 54!

What I do now: Over three decades later and Tina still loves being a Multi Skilled Trades Woman 'on the tools' and a Designer. These combined skill enable her to personally design and create beautiful homes, tailored to suit the clients unique character and lifestyle, helping each one feel wonderful in their beloved environments.

Tina is a Multi Award Winning Tradeswoman, Entrepreneur, Public Speaker, and Construction Industry Role Model, and uses her achievements and visibility to help inspire other women and girls to enter into the trades as a career choice.

Tina is especially passionate about helping disadvantaged women having better lives, training opportunities and career prospects, and so she had set up 'Tools for Life Trade Skills and Welfare Academy Community Interest Company in collaboration with Lisa King. Between the two of them delivering the training at the academy their combined wisdom, empathy and skills will help women to be able to turn their lives around who will undoubtedly go on to become inspirational role model themselves.

How to connect with me:

 www.facebook.com/onthetoolschristina

www.instragram.com/christinamarievalentine/

www.linkedin.com/in/christina-valentinehere

www.pinterest.co.uk/relovedbyvalentine/re-loved-by-valentine/

www.christinavalentine.co.uk

I have a message just for you!
Scan me with your camera or QR app

"Do You think my scarf will remove my vocal cords?"

Talat (Anwer) Cheema-Ahmad

I still remember the last day of school. Everyone bringing in their disposable cameras taking pictures of each other (yep disposable cameras), getting friends and teachers to sign our uniforms that we never ever thankfully have to wear ever again, (my uniform consisted of a bright red jumper with a tree as a logo, and dull grey trousers). Students were throwing flour and eggs around the school premises, girls trying to get their bras up the school flagpole (I went to an amazing all-girls school in south London), and just laughing. Laughing, laughing.. and crying. Those tears carried me all through the summer holidays. It was the end of an era. The best time of my life. And it was over.

Over the summer holidays I was still discovering who I was. 16 years old with my whole life ahead of me. But in a blink of an eye summer was over. It was time to face the music and go to 6th form with new faces. I had butterflies in my stomach. I felt scared, excited and nervous rolled into one.

All my good friends (bar one) moved on to different colleges and left me behind. They laughed at me wanting to stay, but I loved school! I count most of my best years here, the memories, people, teachers, subjects, knowledge, atmosphere, jokes, tears, and laughter. I grew here. I felt like the branches of our school logo, growing and glowing.

I had the best of friends. We were all unique in our own way and yet our bond was something else. We had so much laughter and trust and genuine care for each other. I still remember the first time

I met Danielle when we were about 11-12 years old. She was misbehaving with a pair of scissors with Rochelle. It was debatable as to what she was up to with the scissors but hey, she was always the arty one! (And is now a design illustrator). Danielle was laughing so hard that her forbidden chewing gum flew out of her mouth onto my hand and my initial reaction was to place my forbidden chewing gum onto her hand to be equal! (20 years later she is still one of my best friends, and we both love gum.) School was such an innocent and carefree time. Then just like that after 5 years it was all gone.

I missed them. I *really* missed them, but it was time to start over.

When I went back to school, I did something I hadn't previously done before. I went back into school wearing a headscarf full time. Now that my 6th form was mixed, this was something I wanted to do to represent an element of my identity and my faith. I'm not going to lie, I was absolutely bricking it and I felt like an elephant in the room. *Will people still want to talk to me? Will I make friends? Will they look at me funny?* I was so concerned about people's reaction that for a moment I forgot why I chose to wear it. I knew people would *label* me, and this was my first main adversity in life. Except I was determined to break the stereotype.

On the first day back when I walked into class, I was convinced everyone could hear my heart pounding through my chest. It's like the nerves got the better of me.

Breathe. (I told myself) *Breathe*.

Apart from a handful of numpties, no one really cared what anyone looked like. That's because we were all laughing at something else. Our 6th form had just recently become mixed. So out of about

40 6th formers, 5 of them were boys. Suddenly I didn't feel like the elephant in the room anymore.

There were groups in 6th form/college that I didn't really face in school (or perhaps there were, but because I had my crew I didn't have to think about it). You had to be a certain way to fit into these particular groups.

There was the shy quiet group who always hung out in the computer rooms upstairs battling their low self-esteem, avoiding any attention. A lot of them wore a headscarf. That group was not for me. The loud rebel group that hung downstairs, that wasn't for me. The random leftovers who came from other schools to enrol. That wasn't me. The football obsessed boys who were usually chased by the younger schoolgirls, definitely not for me. *So..where do I go?* Do I join a group based on the stereotyped labels? My best friend Sikisa was in the cool gang, she was my ticket in, but I didn't quite fit in there either.

I kind of learnt to dip in and out of all the rooms, because parts of my identity consisted of all these groups. If anything, I made a lot of friends this way since I did not see their 'label' as a barrier. I began to understand my identity a bit more when I emerged into these different groups.

Different.

Hmm..I'm not sure I quite like the word '*different'* because of what it connotes. But this is *my* story, and I want to use the word '*different'* in a positive light.

Different is good.

Do you remember that lyric from one of Fat boy Slim's songs?

"if everybody looked the same, we'd get tired of looking at each other"

Spot on. This is why I took that leap of faith by stepping out of my comfort zone and allowing the old and new people around me to see another part of my character, the importance faith plays to me through a headscarf. Yet at the same time still holding onto things that are dear to me. My love for ice-skating, my love for music, my love for the arts, games and films (my love for James Bond!), my love for nature and all things green! Most importantly my love for my friends and family.

More and more I began to realise my identity wasn't quite fixed as I thought it should be. I was beginning to let go of labels and judgements even if those around me couldn't.

I did have conversations with friends who would say things like "oh I saw you were sitting with *them* today?" Yes, I was. What's wrong with *them* I thought. I think deep down a lot of people do that. We judge people on what's on the outside without getting to know what's on the inside. We hold this stereotype of something that is *different* to what we are used to or feel comfortable with.

There's that word again. *'different'.* Let me highlight something. *Different* is good. When you allow yourself to come to terms with whatever makes you different, you allow yourself to be – well, You! And what draws friendships is people's individuality! I really felt like a magnet drawn to all things different.

One of my favourite quotes about being different comes from Edwin Bailey Elliot:

"By being yourself you put something wonderful in the world that was not there before" – Edwin Elliott

And what makes the world a wonderful place? Diversity. Can it mean that we can still work side by side together? Absolutely.

This reminds me of a time when I was young, and my mum explained to me how differences and diversity go hand in hand. She told me to look at my hands. And she said to me in Urdu:

"look at your fingers. Are they all the same size?"
"no" I replied
"yet they are working alongside each other to make the hands work right?"
"right" I said

She was right. Without me even realising it my mum had planted that seed in my mind that being different is okay. It doesn't stop you from functioning, nor being a part of the greater good in society. Subconsciously the decision to wear a headscarf was with the notion that deep down it will be ok. Optimistically I wanted to believe everyone is good inside and wants to see the bigger picture in working together harmoniously.

To me 6th form was like a box of Quality Street; I didn't necessarily have a favourite, they were all sweet enough for me. I wish I had a favourite though, then it would be easy to fit in and conform with those around me. I wouldn't have to worry about what to wear because I'd wear what the others wore, name brands were all the rage. But I've never liked branded clothes, I never saw the appeal. I rocked out my unknown unnamed branded items, from unknown independent shops, matching my unbranded multicoloured patchwork bag.

That's what I struggled with most during 6th form, the idea that I just didn't quite fit in anywhere. It's something generally I've always struggled with. Being the odd one out. Don't get me wrong I

embraced being different (on the outside). There wasn't anyone who was quirky like me in 6th form, a tomboy with no fashion sense and wore a headscarf. But perhaps deep down I didn't have the confidence to feel accepted by those around me.

I remember a teacher got us to do one of those career tests, answer questions to figure out what you will be when you are older. Guess what I got? A dog groomer. And this was the response I got from her:

*"Never mind, don't aim too high, just make sure you finish school before you have to get married off! *insert cheap chuckle*".*

It wasn't just school that held labels but the outside world too. We were about 2-3 years after the tragic and horrific 9/11 bombings. There was a sense of judgement in the air about Muslims so if anyone wore a headscarf it was seen as a form of oppression and an easy target to pick on.

I still remember when 9/11 was all over the news. I was heartbroken for the world, absolutely heartbroken at what had happened. And then I was also scared of the repercussions for being a Muslim. I remember being in McDonalds with my friends after school one day when a crazy old bat lady had the audacity to come up to me in front of my friends and shout "*you shouldn't be in here looks like you've got a bomb in your bag*" I was only 14. No one stood up for me. So I had to stand up for myself.

I needed to change the narrative that the media was portraying. I can't let people judge me based on that, that is <u>not</u> me! I knew there and then I would not be seen as a target board for people to throw their judgements or abuse at me based on stereotypes. No one should have to take that. As defensive as I was beginning to feel, I was not going to hide behind a brick wall.

This is why it's important that everyone who has a story should share it. This way, the more narrative you are exposed to as a reader, then the more readers are exposed to gaining a better understanding of *real* people and being able to make their own opinion, rather than allowing the media to make one for them.

Over the next year I allowed myself to let go of trying to figure out who I was and where I fit in. Instead I began to change the perspective, you see fitting in doesn't necessarily give you acceptance, but making a difference gains you something better than that, it gives you a sense of purpose, confidence and accomplishment.

I remember a conversation I had with Sikisa. We had both previously been leaders of the school council and so we held the reputation '*if someone's going to do it, they will!*'.

Sikisa: So.. it's our last year.. what shall we do?
Talat: Something big.
Sikisa: Yeah something big, and meaningful.
Talat: How about a 6th form talent show for the whole school to watch? And the money we raise from the entrance fee can go towards charity?
Sikisa: Perfect!

We both decided to take part in the show as performers. Sikisa formed a group and they choreographed an outstanding dance to *Missy Elliot- 'lose control'*. (By the way skipping forwards by about 15 years, Sikisa went on to become a solicitor by day, and a comedian AND part time artful dancer by night. So, when they said don't aim too high. Don't listen. The sky is your limit.)

I wanted to sing '*All my life'- by Casey and Jo Jo* with Rondella. We shared a mutual love of singing. We went through so many

songs but when we landed on this choice, the words and rhythm complimented our voices and it allowed us to try a range of notes, from the soft tones to the high belters. It was a good choice to show off our range and drum up some attention.

When I had announced I was going to take part and sing, I had a few shocked faces.

"Are you going to sing with your scarf on?"

I froze. I felt vulnerable. To me this question felt like an attack on my identity. Then I laughed and said:

"Do you think my scarf will remove my vocal cords?"

She got embarrassed and laughed it off. But her words were stuck in my head for the rest of that day. I asked myself…*why shouldn't I sing*? That discreet judgement was in the air. *How dare a Muslim sing? Can she even sing? Is she even allowed to sing? Isn't it against her religion?*

I never saw wearing a headscarf as a sign of weakness, if anything it brought out my confidence. I was more determined to show those around me that anything you can do; I can do better. Don't pigeonhole me based on a stereotype. This bit of material covering my head has nothing to do with anyone else but my relationship with God. Something that is personal to *me*. One of *many* strands to *my* identity.

I remember reading a quote by Angelina Jolie that me smile. She said:

"The sun doesn't lose its beauty when its covered by the clouds. The same way your beauty doesn't fade when being covered by hijab"

I was about to reveal a whole lot of sunshine.

We charged 50p as the entrance fee and raised just over £200. The hall was so packed that Mr Gibbs had to physically barricade the door because there was no room for any more students, and the younger years were screaming outside wanting to come in and watch.

Everyone who took part absolutely smashed it and was fantastic! We had dancers, singers, bands, even a comedy act. The hall went crazy it was such a buzz!! When Sikisa went on stage with her crew the lights in the hall went out. The beat of the bass kicked in and the vibrations were felt from the ground. Everyone was nodding their head to the beat of the music without even realising it. Then the lights went on, the crowd went WILD, there were cartwheels, fist bumps, two steps, synchronisation, you name it! it was a very cleverly devised dance routine that won the crowd over! I clapped so hard for her that my hands physically began to hurt and went red. Then it was my turn to get up, walk on stage and perform our duet. There went my pounding chest. *Breathe* (I told myself). For a split second all those judgemental questions raced through my head, *(Can she sing? Is she allowed to sing? Isn't it against her religion? Are you going to sing with your scarf on?).*

Now I've done public speaking before and the advice I constantly follow to calm my nerves is to look into the empty seats when I am talking, because it looks like I'm talking directly at the audience. However, in this case there were no empty seats! I had to bite the bullet. I took a deep breath, fixed my crown (my scarf) by flicking one side of my scarf over my right shoulder, held my head up, walked on stage and opened my mouth to sing.

Everyone went nuts. In a good way! "WHAAAATTTT!!!!" "GURL

YOU CAN SINNNGGG!". I don't think it could have gone any better. We did our good deed and raised money for a children's charity, we got to show case our talents, I got to show everyone I can sing AND wear a scarf, and I was beginning to get over my adversity and begin to believe in myself with confidence. It really couldn't have gone any better. Oh wait. It did.

We got scouted (my friend and I who sang). And they wanted us to enter a talent show competition across the schools in Wandsworth Borough. Two of them were invited by staff to our show to watch everyone perform, (we didn't even know about this), and I never forgot his reaction when I sung, (more so because he had one raised white eyebrow and one black eyebrow, so it was hard not to miss his face), he gave me that look *of 'I would not of thought that sound would come out of you'.*

We went on to perform in a nearby school and I invited my parents to come support and watch me. Someone said *"you're inviting your parents…?"* "I thought about it, and I knew why they asked. They assumed my parents would be embarrassed about the whole situation. I went onto explain that its better they watch me doing something I enjoy, and that I include them in things I love, than to hide it behind their backs. If I'm going to get over my adversity of being labelled to act a certain way, then I need to be honest with myself and those around me.

I'm glad they came to watch me. I felt their warmth and I wanted them to see me do something I was enjoying at the time. I'm the first generation to be born and raised here and so our thinking is not always synchronised, but I wanted to include them in my journey. I still remember my parents (especially mum) beaming smile through my performance, (I got my voice from my mum, so I owe her!).

We didn't win but we did get a runner up prize, Nando's vouchers, my dad was well chuffed with this!

I've come to realise the importance of having an open dialogue with loved ones. Family are more supportive than you may give them credit for, it's not like I wanted to pursue a career in music or anything, but I wanted to share this key moment from my teenage years, of how a label almost tried to prevent me from using my voice and ultimately clouding my confidence.

Yet I chose to rise above it with newfound courage. I finally felt confident in who I am, how I am, and how I look. I said it before, but I want to say it again. I never saw, and still don't see how wearing a headscarf is a sign of weakness. It's not, it's empowering, it highlights my confidence. Anything you can do, I *can* do better.

Fast forward years later, I went on to achieve many great things that I am proud of. Just to name a few:

I obtained a BA in Sociology and Cultural studies.
I played for the women's football team at Goldsmith University (with my scarf).
Whilst I was a Student Ambassador, I co-organised an Aspire Student Ambassador Conference with students across 4 different universities (with my scarf). I still have the flyer till this day.

Career wise I didn't become a dog groomer as predicted, nor was I married off before school finished, but I went onto completing my PGCE and NQT and became a secondary school teacher specialising in Citizenship and Design and Technology (with my scarf).

One of my teaching jobs was at an Islamic Independent Girls

School in East London, and with the help of the most inspirational (temporary) Headteacher Mrs F Qazi, we introduced work experience for the very first time and fought to make sure it was made compulsory for all the girls to participate. Hours were spent planning on coordinating work experience places that would take our girls on. It ranged from law to journalism, to teaching to retail etc. I still remember visiting each student from the first batch at their workplaces to see how they were getting on and meeting the staff. Most of all I still remember the feeling and faces of how happy these girls were to be given the opportunity they never thought they would get.

I am also an Entrepreneur under the name of @talatstreats where I make handmade gifts with love for all occasions. This was something that started off as a hobby whilst I was a stay at home mum and then it extended over time with encouragement from my friends.

I am just about to start my own Creative Mums club in Slough whilst I'm also covering a maternity post for the Creative Mums club in Hounslow under Creative Spaces London. But I have to save that for another story.

I've always wanted to show my children that mummy is a hard working multi-tasking woman and that the sky is *your* limit.

I finally figured something out about the word 'identity'. *It is not fixed.* You can actually be whatever you want to be within the right frame, however you want to be or look, don't let anyone take it away from you. You must *believe* in yourself. *You've got this.*

For me getting over my adversity was trying to get over a perceived label of what a Muslim is. The media played a big role in shaping the stereotype. So it was my job to tell you my story and break that narrative. It's not what's on your head that matters, it's

what's on the inside that counts. Its true when they say you should never judge a book by its cover.

I am not your expectation, I make my own expectations.

I am grateful for my family, my upbringing, my roots, my faith, my friends, my culture, my surroundings, my experiences, my determination and my kind heart. All of that combined has made me who I am today. You have to be willing to be put in the hard work to see it pay off. And remember. Don't give up. You've got this!

It might not feel like it, but sometimes overcoming adversity is a bit of a blessing in disguise, in the sense that, it's a learning curve and a taught lesson of all the bigger and better things to come.

I have 2 beautiful young daughters of my own now. I feel it's partly my purpose to guide them and encourage them to create their own futures. Their story isn't written yet, and that's up to them to finish their narratives and tell you one day.

For now, I hope who ever reads this draws strength from my story. I've faced discrimination, I've faced judgement, I knew I was different. But I like being different. It made me strong, it gave me courage, it made me determined and it gave me hope that I can make a change. I worked hard and I did things people didn't think I could do just because of who I am, not what I am.

But you see, I am me, and I am proud of me and all I have achieved, (and I hope my girls are proud of me too).

I sincerely hope someday you can achieve your dreams too.

Author: Talat (Anwer) Cheema-Ahmed

A quirky fact about me: I am an adrenalin junky at heart! I've done done a bungee jump in Windsor, Jungle Ziplining in Thailand, horse ride in Pakistan, and a Swing over the Rice fields in Bali. I've only got one life, I have to make the most of it.

What I do now: Using her experience of being a Teacher and a Mother, Talat Co runs empowering workshops for Mums (under Creative Spaces London) implementing creativity, art and group coaching. The sessions are there to help remind these women that they are more than 'just a mum' but they are AMAZING and more! The aim is also to help and encourage mums back on their feet with what ever direction they wish to embark upon within a safe space. These sessions are supported and surrounded by the love and encouragement of other mums and facilitators. For fun, Talat also runs a small business from home making hand made gifts and party favours using her passion of creativity.

How to connect with me:

www.facebook.com/talatstreats

www.instagram.com/talatstreats

I have a message just for you!
Scan me with your camera or QR app

"Why Don't You Love Me?"

Nilam Dattani

Have you ever had a time in our life where you have waited to hear the answer to a question.? For you, it may have been a hospital test result or perhaps it was an exam result or even the result of a job interview.

As she waited for the answer, she repeated the question in her head: "Why don't you love me?"

And then the answer came like a freight train... "What is there to love about you! You're fat, you're ugly, you're a useless worthless piece of shit! "

Have you ever wanted to get a different answer, maybe even asked the question differently? She was the same, but every time the answers were always the same. She felt so unloved, she had no confidence left in her and everyday life just seemed such a chore. She became a shadow of her former self, unable to go places on her own, feeling like everyone was looking at her, staring, mocking her. Days turned into weeks, weeks turned into months, time moved on, but for her… the insecurities grew, the tears flowed at the drop of a hat. All she wanted was to feel loved.

Have you ever wanted to feel loved?

At the age of Forty-Eight, she had felt unloved for most of her adult life, not worthy and not good enough. So why was she so unhappy? Throughout life, like many of you, she faced challenges

that had a direct impact on her. Now, if life didn't have challenges, no up's and down's, then life would get a little boring right? However, to her, these up's and down's felt like tidal waves at best and a full-on Tsunami at worst, as her challenges just kept coming and coming, one after the other.

No sooner had she dusted herself off and got back on her feet again, then WHAM there came another. She began to take everything personally, the way someone spoke to her or looked at her, she would read between the lines and hear something different to what was actually being said, making up her own shite, in her own shitty little world.

Here she stood staring at her attacker;

The woman standing in front of her, 5ft 2" shoulder length dark silky soft hair, big brown eyes. She watched her thinking… if only I had what she had, vibrant, fun-loving, drop-dead gorgeous with a swarm of people around her. A giving and loving person, always ready to help others. Even the mention of her name and what it meant caused a pang of pain. You see, in her culture, the name holds the meaning of a 'precious blue stone', vibrant, strong, a symbol of endurance, stability the ability to be grounded and connected.

The woman's brown eyes looked right back of me, how could she look so like me and yet be so different?

I felt none of those characteristics, I felt the total opposite, dull, weak, unstable and disconnected. I saw a lonely, ugly, fat thing with a complex as big as her arse, that I wasn't good enough for anyone or anything. I had reached a point in my life where I felt the world and everyone in my life would be better off without me. I was at the lowest I had ever felt, I didn't like myself, I didn't see any

value or worth about myself. My mind was full of all the reasons why everyone would benefit if I wasn't here. I would wake up put on my makeup and wear a fake smile, trying to convince the world that I was okay and living my best life. I knew I wanted to be different, I wanted to feel different. I longed to be 'me' again, I was tired and fed up of feeling like crap.

And yet as I looked at my reflection in the mirror, I knew the hurtful, harmful words that I said to myself every day were never going to help me. I wanted to change but I didn't know how.

Layton my fiancé, who is tall, strong and Scottish, tried to help as best he could, being caring, loving, and so very supporting. He said all the right things, positive, encouraging, kind and considerate words. He believed in me and saw in me more than I ever did.

Have you ever heard the saying … 'you can't help someone until they are ready to help themselves?

That's exactly what I intended to do, help myself. I began, to realise that my "mood' was having an impact on Layton, my boys and relationships and friendships around me. Layton's support and love was everything to me and I feared driving him away, into the arms of someone else, someone who treated him better than me. It was like looking in on myself and I could see my attitude and behaviour was not what I wanted it to be.

I would hear my dad's guiding voice saying to me "Mataji (meaning princess, as he would often call me) it's all about mind over matter, you can do this you have the strength, find it". And so, It was now or never.

It was January 2019 and like the rest of the world, I was full of

hope for the year ahead. I was going to make this year my year! Out with the old and in with the new. I wanted life to be different, I want to be happier, I wanted to be me again. I was fed up with the same old feeling of sadness and emptiness, waking up in the morning with no spring in my step and that dread of what lies ahead, you know what I'm talking about right?

Everyone has a New Year resolution list of goals. I had mine. A list of goals that often fizzled out because “A goal without a plan or a timeline is just a wish,” I did neither. I wanted to be fitter, I wanted to look better and I wanted to be happier.

Have you noticed how all these “wants’ are external things, everything that impacts the outside of me?

The only thing that I stuck to, was my fitness, many of you probably couldn’t find anything worse to do but for me it made me feel good, I got a sense of achievement even from the small wins. I could see my progress from the measurements and pictures I was taking, you see... tracking my progress made it visible to see the change. Seeing the change was a real reminder of my journey, where I was versus where I am. And that’s so important to do.

Do you track any of your goals or journey?

Around February 2019 a Facebook advert kept popping up on my timeline, the strapline was “The most empowering thing you can do...is to love yourself.” It was Valentines time, a time of love. It caught my eye it was like it was speaking directly to me because it knew how I felt about myself. I clicked on the link and it took me to a page called ‘Smart Photography’. A beautiful picture of a sassy dressed woman, was centre shot on the page, “wow! she looks stunning” I thought. The woman was not what I expected, she had a more fuller frame than most and absolutely beautiful “if she can

then I can." I was envious that she had the confidence to have such pictures taken, and I began to feel inadequate and clicked off the page. Here's the thing... I didn't like having my picture taken. The image stayed on my mind, I couldn't get over how much beauty, class and sassiness oozed out of the picture. I wanted to look like that! I wanted to be the one in the picture, to feel exactly what the picture portrayed, class, sass and beauty.

That little voice within made itself heard... "you, looking like that, are you having a laugh you're fat and you're ugly." The dream only lasted for a few minutes, and that's all it was a dream...

Have you ever wanted to look as good as someone else? I couldn't remember the last time I felt good about myself, it seemed like years.

It was almost April, a couple of months after seeing the advert the first time. The advert kept popping up, like Facebook was listening to my inner desires, or was it the universe hearing my cry for help. Every time it popped up, I browsed a little deeper, admiring all the stunning pictures of all those women brave enough to bare their bodies. I had a gut instinct that I needed to do this, I just had a knowing that this was the right thing for me to start my journey into self-love. There were times I started to fill in the contact form only to allow that inner voice to do its magic and talk me out of it.

I had mentioned to a colleague on a few occasions that I had come across this advert and what it was all about. She kept telling me to go for it and that I'd look beautiful in them, but I didn't believe her, she could've told me until I was blue in the face it wouldn't have made a difference until I believed it myself. Until one day... whilst at work it popped up again, WTF had I done!! I was stood there with my phone in my hand shaking, my palms sweaty, my heart was beating so hard I could hear it echoing in the room.

"Whoooosshhhh" the contact form was sent! If you could've seen me, I would have looked like the emoji of the monkey covering its eyes crossed with the green emoji feeling sick. There was no way of retrieving the form, it was on its way waiting to be assessed.

I walked back into the office, over to my desk, my colleague who sat opposite me looked at me in concern. "what's wrong, what's happened?" "I erm… I've just sent that form off, the one for the photoshoot," "oh my gosh Nilam!! I thought something really bad had happened" "it has!" "don't be stupid," she said laughing, "well done you, how exciting." There it went again that voice, 'You, stupid fat b**ch, you're going to make such a fool of yourself hahahahaha!' At the same time, there was excitement, I didn't even realise I had filled in the form until after… everything happens for a reason, right? It must do.

Have you had a moment where you had taken a leap of faith, stepped out of your comfort zone feeling scared yet so excited, or are you still waiting to but can't?

A week later, whilst out for dinner with Layton, my phone rang. It was a number from the area where the studio was, a place called Witney in Oxfordshire. I started to feel nervous, I stared at my phone hoping it would stop, it seemed to ring for ages. I told him it was a 0800 number and then messaged the number back explaining I couldn't take the call, and would it be ok if to arrange a time and date to talk.

I hadn't told Layton what I had done, I didn't want to tell him either. Not because it was a secret or because I kept things from him. Because I wanted to do this for myself, it wasn't about taking photo's dressed in lingerie for him, it was about doing this for me! Probably the most important thing I had ever done for myself, at the time I didn't realise the true impact this would have on me.

The phone rang, it was that number again… my heart began to race, for two reasons. On one hand, I wanted to ignore it, afraid of what was to come and on the other, I was intrigued and excited. I answered it gingerly barley getting my voice out

"Hello?"
"Hiii Nilam, how are you?"

Her voice was so warm and friendly, almost instinctively knowing I'd be nervous. I thought I was the only one in the world who was apprehensive, but Anna quickly reassured me that almost everyone felt anxious and nervous. Anna put my mind at ease very quickly, she asked why I wanted to do the shoot. Tears began to flow I had a lump in my throat it was hard to talk about how I felt about myself and why I felt I was where I was.

Anna explained the process thoroughly, she asked if I had any questions, no I had all info I needed. Oh, shite!! I had done it again before I knew it, I had booked a date for the shoot and had paid my £50 non-refundable deposit. This time picture the monkey hiding emoji with the being sick emoji only this time there's also the pile of poo emoji! There's no going back now… I didn't tell Layton the date, I didn't tell him anything. I had to think of an excuse, so I told him, I was going for lunch with a colleague. He didn't believe, he knew something wasn't right.

The day before I was going, I told him, he was worried that I had signed up to go somewhere that wasn't safe… I assured him it was and agreed for him to come along to keep his mind at ease, but he had to wait in the car after the initial booking in.

The place was small, the walls were decorated with different styles of pictures, some were very revealing yet sexy and tasteful, fair play to them I thought. Anna did a fab job again at easing my mind

and she took me through different styles of photos asking which ones I was ok with. I was in awe of those ladies in the pictures, no matter what shape or size they all looked amazing. There were so many different styles, a simple bra and knicker set, lingerie, body/teddy suits. Some had everyday clothing on like sheer tops or their partners' shirt. Then, there was the more risqué ones, dominatrix gear, leather and bondage gear. I wasn't brave enough to say yes to those! However, there was one that really spoke to me, it was a mirror image naked silhouette, it looked absolutely stunning! That one was a maybe on the list.

It was time to go in, Layton went back to the car and I was taken through with my suitcase full of clothes. As I entered the room, I saw the photographer. In my overwhelm, I forgot it was a man, Anna's husband, Robin. I needn't have worried though he was brilliant! I got my hair and makeup done I felt a million dollars. Robin chatted to keep my mind busy and I soon forgot I was almost naked in front of a stranger.

The room had a deep red chaise lounge at one end of the room and a large bed at the other dressed in white, there were a few props on the bed too like feathers and flowers. Having seen the photo's of others beforehand, I had an idea of how the furniture and props would come in to play. As we went through wardrobe changes and poses, I began to enjoy the session, bearing in mind I didn't like pictures of me being taken. So doing this semi-naked was a huge deal.

And then came that question, "Nilam are you ready to do the nudes?" Ohhh, I felt sick. I had a voice sitting on either shoulder. "Go on girl! You've come this far, if you don't, you'll regret it" "You can't do that! It's culturally wrong to stand naked in front of another man, what will Layton think? I wanted to text him to get his opinion, but I needed to make this decision for myself. And so, the decision

was yes! I bared my ass, as some would say.

Three hours later it was all done, as I walked back to the car I was hit with this wave of emotion, I couldn't stop crying. "What's happened," Layton asked fearing the worst. "Babe, please don't be angry I feel like I've betrayed you" You can imagine what went through his mind! "I did the nudes, I'm so sorry" "Sorry, what on earth for? I'm not angry, I'm bloody proud of you!!" With that, he gave me the biggest, tightest hug, and I too felt proud of myself. Are you proud of yourself for your achievements?

Two weeks later just after my Forty-Seventh birthday, It was time to go and review the pictures. I wasn't anxious or nervous I was excited. I told my boys what I had done, they gave money to go towards the pictures as a birthday gift. I entered the viewing room and Layton followed a few minutes after. I sat down on the sofa and as I looked up there was a mahoosive picture of me on an easel.

I was dressed or undressed, in a white matching lingerie set. I have never seen myself in that way before, I was so overwhelmed. it wasn't the fact that I was semi-naked It, was because I looked beautiful. "Is that me?" I asked through a river of tears. "yes, that's you" said Elise the assistant. "Really… that's me?" "Yes," she said smiling. Just then Layton walked in, "Wow! These are incredible" He was still stood near the door and as I looked towards him, I clocked the wall with rows of pictures of me. Twenty Six! to be precise and I had walked straight past them. How did I not see them? They were all of me…I wasn't expecting to see them all on display, It was a little intimidating and embarrassing. I was being hit with waves of mixed emotions, I didn't know what I was feeling or thinking. It felt surreal, an outer body experience, watching myself going through this journey of self-discovery. I was a wreck, struck with surprise, gobsmacked with belief and totally overcome

with pride and love for myself. Layton tried to get me over to have a look at them, I was stuck to the sofa, I couldn't bring myself to go over, I don't know why I can't really remember. After a bit of coaxing, I did, we looked at each one and exchanged thoughts on which ones we liked the best individually.

We were then shown a slide show of them on the TV. Flippin' hell they were all me! And there it was, my favourite one, the nude mirror reflection, I did it!! For the first time in my life, I liked what I saw. So much so I ended up buying all of them. They were quite expensive, but I thought, it's taken me Forty-Seven years to say I like myself, to be able to look in the mirror without disgust. If I divided the cost by forty-seven (years) it was just a smidge under £100 over a twelve-month payment plan, yes work out the maths!

In the weeks that followed people noticed new confidence, and I could look at myself without hate and dissatisfaction. My photo's appeared on their Instagram page, my son was sharing them on his page. I was buzzing with pride seeing myself out there on the worldwide social media platforms. Layton showed a couple of females at his work to inspire them after they had shared with him how they had no self-confidence. I felt empowered with a huge sense of achievement.

This was the beginning of my self-development journey and it wasn't the only significant action I did to help myself. Although I had this new air of confidence, I still felt stuck. The biggest thing for me was losing my dad 6 years earlier, moving away from London leaving my boys, my friends and network and my job of 15 years all within a space of two weeks. The accumulative loss and grief consumed my entire being and soul like the Grim Reaper was ready to take my place. All I could feel was deaths despair while the rest of my emotions and feelings lay dormant. I was on the edge of handing my life over to the Grim Reaper but at the same

time, I was hoping for a miracle because deep down I wanted to stay alive, I wanted to be happy living my best life. And that miracle came…I met Lisa King a co-author of this book at the same time as I met the Grim Reaper. Lisa recommended therapy as my grief resonated with her, I went on to have Rapid Transformational Therapy (RTT) with Cheryl Chapman co-founder of the 'Find Your Why Foundation'. RTT helped me to release hidden traumas. Trauma that had been keeping me stuck and snowballed over my Forty Seven years. My life has changed, I have changed, I have found 'ME'!

Throughout my life, I have faced all sorts of challenges that attributed to my insecurities, a lack of self-worth and no self-love. Now, many of you would have faced challenges in your life too, and everyone's challenges affect them in different ways and that's ok! Don't compare your life to someone else's, if you face the same challenge as someone else, their journey will take them on a different path to you. Do challenges break you, initially maybe, but they are so good at helping you grow. You can learn so much about yourself from them, use them to grow, Seek the help that you know will help you to overcome them. This isn't a journey you can do alone and it's ok to ask for help.

How good does it feel when you're asked to help someone? … So, by not asking for help are you denying that person of feeling good? of course, you are!

You have one life, live it in a way that makes you happy, smile from within and the world will smile with you. Don't compromise your inner happiness, your inner peace and mind for anything. Love yourself like you love others, respect yourself like you respect others, be kind to yourself like you are kind to others.

Today, I am the happiest I have ever been, I accept myself for who

I am and all that I stand for. I live my life authentically in the way that I want to and not how others tell me I should. I am fulfilling the dreams and desires that I choose. My relationship with food and my mental and physical health has improved now that I have self-love and self-respect. I no longer starve and sacrifice myself when faced with upset or trauma.

I Coach young female adults at a local school, supporting them to build the self-love and self-respect they deserve. I work with entrepreneurs supporting them in their business where they help transform the lives of others.

My relationships are healthier and balanced because having self-love means that I'm not constantly double guessing and doubting words from others.

In Layton's words, *"Our relationship is stronger than ever, we stand together strong as a team, and all of this has come because Nilam has taken ownership of her life. I'd say her self-love has been at the core of her transformation. From the first day, I met her, I always believed there was a beautiful power within her. I am super proud to see she now acknowledges and believes in her greatness too."*

And finally, before I love you and leave you, I'd like you to spend a few minutes thinking about the following...

Have you ever wanted to feel loved?
Love yourself first, look in the mirror, look yourself in the eye and say "I love you" at least twice a day. When you wake and before you go to bed.

Have you ever heard the saying ... 'you can't help someone until they are ready to help themselves?

Think about the areas in your life that you want support with?

Have you noticed how all these "wants' are external things, everything that impacts the outside of me?
Nourish your mind and body by focusing on the internal care first. Treat yourself with the love, care and respect you deserve.

Have you ever wanted to look as good as someone else?
Why? When you already have all that richness and beauty within yourself. Remember to tell yourself "I love you."

Have you had a moment where you had taken a leap of faith, stepped out of your comfort zone feeling scared yet so excited, or are you still waiting to, but can't?
In the moment of opportunity, the first 5 seconds are crucial, Don't, let those fears, nerves or self-talk stop you from doing things that you want to. Say yes to it and then figure out the how and when. Cease the moment don't live with regret.

Do you track any of your goals or journey?
Journaling is a positive way to start your day, creating a daily routine of self-affirmations, daily intentions and goal setting. A way to visually see your thoughts and overcome them, build up the confidence and belief within. Start with at least 3 affirmations every day. Affirmations are self-praise and a way to bring to your awareness all the great attributes about yourself, for example,

"I am ENOUGH" "I am BEAUTIFUL" "I am AMAZING"

"You, yourself, as much as anybody in the entire universe, deserve your love and affection" – Buddha

Are you ready to take back your life and live it with purpose?

Author: Nilam Dattani

A quirky fact about me: Nilam was an Indian Classical Dance performer when she was younger

What I do now: Nilam is one of the Co-Creators and an Author of this book, and wanted to create this book as an opportunity to help and inspire others who are facing or have faced similar challenges as the authors.

Nilam coaches teenagers and adults to overcome challenges which are stopping them from being their authentic self.

Nilam also supports Entrepreneurs and Small Business owners to organise and run their activities and events as well as their online services.

She is a Facilitator with the 'Find Your Why Foundation' which is a collaborative, creative community which helps Women to become more #FrikkinAwesome.

Nilam also supports the 'Clarity, Focus and Growth Collective Group' which supports individuals to Break Barriers and Limitations in order to achieve success.

Nilam believes that to get the most of out life, you have to show up with Authenticity, Positive Intention and a high level of Self-awareness, enabling you to understand your own character, emotions, feelings and reactions to everyday events, which in turn will ultimately allow you to make better decisions in your life.

Nilam believes that personal transformation is never complete and always striving to become the best version of you gives a life full of excitement, inner peace and continuous purpose.

How to connect with me:

 https://www.facebook.com/nilam.dattani211/

 https://www.findyourwhyfoundation.com/

 https://www.facebook.com/groups/clarityfocusandgrowth/

 @nils_livelovelife

 nilam211@gmail.com

 nilam@findyourwhyfoundation.com

I have a message just for you!
Scan me with your camera or QR app

Scarcity to Abundance

Mir Kamran Ali

It was a hot summer, schools were off due to summer break. One day I asked my mother to buy me an ice cream, but my mother replied to me that "we cannot afford to have ice cream," as an 8-year-old boy it was difficult to understand what could be the reason. I always used to ask a lot of "why" questions, so I asked my mother "Ammi but why I cannot have ice cream? Why all my friends can have it? Why all my cousins have it? My mother replied and explained the real situation, "Your father has lost his job, he lost his investment and we have limited source of income, you should be grateful to God that you are in school and have enough food every day, and have your grandparent's house to live in".

When I see that I was not getting what other kids used to have, I used to get an inferior complex, I felt that that we are below other people and we are not up to other peoples standards. It triggered me in such a way that I needed to do something to improve the situation for my family, and I wanted to remove this scarcity from my life.

Time passed on and I finished my school 10th year. One day I went to my friends home for joint studies, sharing notes and I saw a quote on the mirror in his room which said, "The road to success is always under construction. It is a progressive course, not an end to be reached." "What! I asked him, what does it mean?" "Where does this come from?" He said it was from the famous author

Tony Robbins. It came from the book called Unlimited Power. This quote really made me think that I was missing something.

I felt like I found the solution to deal with my life. I could overcome my scarcity and could turn things around. What could be the right thing that I needed to be a successful person? I was a dreamer from my childhood, I always used to say that I will achieve huge things, but I was suppressed and most of the time people used to laugh at me, at my ideas and my dreams. Of course, I was not in the right group or surroundings.

I decided to learn more about it. But I did not know how it worked, what was the secret that I needed to know? How to achieve success? I was in Pakistan, which was an underdeveloped country, and I did not have a computer or access to the internet. I used to get only one schoolbook. I became so eager to learn that I asked my friend to tell me what the book said. He then gave me the chapter summaries which I used to memorise in my mind. I gradually started to observe, how does this work?

But things were getting tough for me. My father got made redundant suddenly when I was still young, he could not manage a better job. Things got even worse when he invested his redundancy money into some money return schemes, but the project was a huge loss. We became hand to mouth, we were living with other uncles and aunts in my grandfather's house as a joint family, which was quite normal in Pakistan. We were going through such hardship that it was difficult to even buy clothes. We never talked about it as my mother always taught us that things will change when you pay gratitude towards God, regardless of the

situation. We really learnt how to appreciate what we had, even when life was so hard.

Academically I was doing well. So, I started to use my teaching skills and started to give maths tuition privately at an early age to earn some money to cover my expenses. As time passed by, I took admission to the university to learn physiotherapy.

Things were looking promising. It was three years of Bachelor's degree, which was upgraded up to a 4 year programme which was even better. That upgrade was not authorised by the education committee though and the student union then went on strike. As a result, the first semester, which was supposed to be completed within one year, did not happen for 2 years. There was a lot of frustration amongst the students, many students dropped out due to uncertainty. I was losing hope for my future, I was getting depressed with the situation. I was a good student with high ambitions and big dreams but the system and delays caused a lot of frustrations and depression.

I was getting frustrated as there was no certainty with when my degree was going to finish, so I decided to study computers in the evenings so that my time was not wasted. I then took part time admission to a computer course.

After two years of struggle, the education commission approved the course to be a four year degree programme and all the semester was rearranged. Then the exam was conducted and finally, I completed my Bachelors Degree in Physiotherapy and at the same time I also completed my computer diploma.

Then I started to look for jobs. I wished to join the same hospital where I was studying. It was a good hospital with a particularly good reputation, but I was not selected for an internship, even

though I was exceptionally good academically. There were politics and favouritism going on and the system was corrupt. This is quite common in Pakistan, that jobs are offered based on connection and political affiliations, merits are over looked. I felt rejected; I was depressed and sad with the system, where hard work and talent does not get appreciated.

I kept on looking for jobs in different places and managed to get a job in a university hospital, which was situated on the outskirts of the city. It took me around 6 hours a day to travel to and from work which was not working for me either.

I kept trying to manage an internship at another hospital, which was one of the famous hospitals in Pakistan but there was no luck. However, I did not give up. It seems to me that Law of Attraction was working for me and during the graduation I met the manager of that hospital and I went to speak to him. I expressed to him that I was trying to get an appointment to apply for a job but was not getting any chance to meet him. I also explained that I had submitted my CV several times but there was no response. He told me, “Yeah, you can come to my office.” He gave me an appointment! “Yay….I did it! I felt great…”.

But when I went there, he said “you can join as a volunteer.” as that was the only post available at that time. I felt that even after such long studies this is how I am treated, with no respect and no appreciation of merit. Any way I agreed and started working there. I worked initially as a volunteer and was later offered an internship. The internship was low paid and it hardly covered my travel expenses. This continued for six months and in that time, I started some other work to maintain my expenses. The dream was big, and I was not losing my hope, I wanted to do so much more. By this time, I was working extremely hard.

I started giving services as a freelancer in IT and computers, I started to build up my profile with the clients and solving problems for big companies. My pay was low as I was a new individual, but my quality of service was excellent. Word of mouth spread, and I got a contract to develop software for international companies like Siemens Pakistan and Wackenhut Securities. I got an offer for a job in physiotherapy, but the condition was I had to take full time hours on a part time salary. That was the way to get a full-time job at that time and I was so desperate that I accepted, and continued for a year or so. I continually requested that the manager should promote me to full time, as I have been working there for so long with no salary change, and I was getting frustrated and losing my self worth.

This was not working for me and I wanted to do something better, so I decided to take a higher degree from abroad. I thought I would get a better position and better rate of pay after finishing it. I started to search for universities, it was another stressful time for me as getting an admission abroad was not easy with such high fees and living expenses.

Dealing with all those limitations meant that the earning potential was limited too and I needed a lot of money to go abroad to pay fees, for the university, plane ticket, accommodation etc. The currency rates were out of my control, the university fees for the foreign students were higher too, but I dreamt big, so I started to work harder.

In addition to work I started to provide more IT services, taking on private patients for an extra income in the evenings, I was also working in a call centre. I kept going, as I knew I could achieve it, I had no support from anybody, but my dream and hunger to achieve was there. Finally, I managed to get the money together, and, I got an approval from the University of East London in the UK.

I came to the UK in 2006 and started my study for post-graduation. After completing my studies I decided to get married and I married a lady who I had known for many years.

My financial crisis did not improve and after University I worked in a small office, extremely low salary and working over 70 hours a week, my employer did not treat me well and I could not see a way out. I then started to read personal development books and started watching some motivational videos. It gave me confidence and I then decided to start my own business. I kept the job and started to sell some products online. I saw the potential in it so I kept going.

I started to put more time and effort into the business and found some good results. I got myself familiarised with the online market place, and gradually I started to grow my inventory, it was a new start and I was learning, gaining experience and experimenting with new things. In addition I started investing my savings and salaries, I wanted to be rich quickly, another setback, I was scammed by a Chinese company and I lost everything that I had earned so far, it was a big failure. I went into depression, I did not want to do anything, go anywhere or talk to anyone.

My wife was so supportive, we decided I should continue with my job, although I really didn't like it, and we will find our way again, at this point we were expecting our first child. Things got worse, credit card debt was increasing, no additional income, we cut our expenses as much as we could, the regret, the burden was increasing.

One night when I was returning from my work, I picked up a Metro newspaper while commuting on the London tube. There was an ad that Tony Robbins is coming to the UK for the first time, to deliver his 'Unleash the Power Within' seminar. I really wanted to

attend, so my wife and I went for the enrolment session. It felt like a blessing and that the Law of Attraction was at work.

As we found out the fee for the seminar, my wife stepped back. The biggest challenge was we did not have enough money to pay for it. So, I spoke to the promoter of the seminar and they agreed to split the payment. My wife said we cannot afford to spend anything extra at this moment. She was right but I was desperate for a change and took a credit card loan for three months.

I was prepared to make some big changes, I made a lot of commitments to myself, I took a lot of notes and looked at what I needed to change, I learnt a lot from the seminar, and I explored the ways I was self- sabotaging and how quickly I could recover from those. I restarted the business again in a different way with a different strategy and with better research.

At this time we had a baby girl, we moved to a bigger place, as I needed more space to work. I reinvested some money, while still paying off outstanding credit cards, things started to progress, we were more organised, we were seeing good results, the debts were being paid off and I formed a Limited company. My wife helped too while I was at work during the day, we were gaining experience, taking calculated risks, even hiring storage for our inventory.

My job was taking its toll on me, the stress of the long hours and the lack of appreciation, even when I was working on a huge project and getting no extra money. Once the business could cover expenses I could quit the job. We had decided to move and get a bigger home, one that could also serve the business better, so we decided to move out of London, we moved to Nottingham. In addition my employers attitude was now unacceptable and this was the trigger I needed to leave my London job and focus on my

own business full time. I felt free, like a huge weight had been lifted off my shoulders.

It was a very big jump. I was all pumped up working full time on my business and I believed I could take it to the next level. That attitude helped me a lot and my focus was loud and clear. I continued investing my heart and soul in to the business and I created various streams of income. From IT services, helping businesses grow, my products expanded and I started getting contracts with the suppliers and distributors. I started to contact different auction houses, warehouses to secure better deals. My product range and variety grew, my profit margin got better. Within one year of leaving the job, there was a substantial growth in the business which was like three times the earnings of the job.

It was a good decision to leave the job, to leave the toxic people who did not value me. Business was doing well, and of course, business never stays the same, there are ups and downs. One thing I have made sure is that I have continued to work on myself, making positive changes, working on self-development and business development.

Today I am grateful that I am an Entrepreneur who changed my state of scarcity to abundance. Today I provide services to develop businesses, I am a Social Media Marketing Adviser, I develop business IT network solution, I provide cloud services, I develop websites, I develop customised software, I am a Coach for Business Development, I am an Online Retailer, I am an Online Brand Ambassador for a famous international brand, I am a Book Designer, I am a T-shirt Designer. I am Cost Draftsman for legal firms (this skill I learned from my previous job).

I must say that dreams do come true when you work hard and

persevere, and yes it can take time to reach your destination or desired goal. Now, not only am I benefitting, I am also able to help others. Today I give huge gratitude to God and to people who are in my life, and those who are no longer in my life, who have helped me to achieve what I wanted to achieve.

Now I look at my two daughters and want to give them a better start to progress themselves, so they too can help others and keep the legacy going.

This is the advice I always give to everyone, “be persistent”, “never give up” and “believe in yourself”. One day you will get there….

Love and gratitude to my mother for raising me in such a manner.

Author: Mir Kamran Ali

A quirky fact about me: I am passionate about the ecosystem and greenery and healthier a environment.

What I do now: Kamran Ali is an online entrepreneur who specialises in Online Retailing and Ecommerce Business. Kamran provides System Solutions to businesses with their IT Infra Structure, Website Development, Mobile Application Development and Networking.

Kamran also provides services in Social Media, Graphic Designing including T-shirt and Print Media. Kamran is a Business Coach foe selling physical products online.

How to connect with me:

www.facebook.com/mirkamranali

@mirkamran.ali

www.linkedin.com/in/mirkamranali/

@MirKamranAli

@mirkamranali

I have a message just for you
Scan me with your camera or QR app

“Today I choose to live by choice”

Janine Dunn

Have you ever heard the saying…life is full of choices?

It’s Monday 7th January 2002, it’s the day of choices.

Here I am sitting on a two-seater, dark brown faux leather type sofa, in a small, windowless room, about the size of the small box bedroom of a 3-bedroom house. The bright fluorescent strip lighting above me is hurting my eyes. There are the sounds of many muffled voices and the familiar ever-present undertone of a stomach-churning, nauseating chemical smell. Opposite me is my mum, sitting on another two-seater, dark brown faux leather type sofa.

Mum is 5ft 1” with short styled black and grey hair. She is a kind, caring, generous, fiercely loyal woman, with solid integrity. Who underneath the consequential mental health issues, that she has had to bear from all the pressures, all the challenges, all the choices that have come from all the lemons in life thrown at her and our family over the years, has a cheeky, quick witted and mischievous sense of humour. She reminds me a bit like a mix of the serious Annette Crosbie from One Foot in The Grave and of the quick witted, cheeky and mischievous Celia Imrie from The Calendar Girls film.

My sister, Michelle, is sitting to the right-hand side of me on the sofa. She has long brunette hair to her shoulders and looks a lot like my mum, albeit an extra 2 inches taller.

"Ah, here he is!", I say to myself. A tall man, about 6ft, with dark hair, enters the room. His face a blur, as my eyesight shuts off with the sound of his words shooting into my eardrums like an exploding bullet...

..."I'm really sorry, there is nothing we can do. The ventilator is doing the breathing for him, as he has suffered a massive brain haemorrhage and he is showing no signs of brain activity in trying to breathe on his own."

As the words start to spin in my head, I hear the voices in my head..."WHY did I go home and leave him in the cubicle in A&E alone? I knew something was not quite feeling right and we NEVER do this as a family. I could've stayed, I could've slept in the chair next to him and let the others go home for some rest. I know mum relies on me, as she says, you are the one in the family that understands all this medical stuff. If only you had stayed with him! Then you would have noticed him before he had a stroke and got him treatment straightaway...now, it's too late!"

See Dad and I had set out on what I can only liken to a triathlon. We did all the researching and putting all the hard work and effort, into making sure he was fit for action, by preparing and eating all the foods to boost him with superfoods.

The first event we entered, was the back and forth to the hospital each day for Chemotherapy. The second event, being the back and forth for Radiotherapy. Dad was in the lead of this triathlon, he was winning the battle of shrinking the tumour in his lung wrapped around his aorta, despite being on palliative care combinations and to the surprise of the Oncologist. We were in the last event of the triathlon together now, the hurdles. We had jumped and cleared each hurdle on the triathlon circuit, with the last one winning hurdle

in Dad's sight, when Whoosh!! BANG!!

"Why are all eyes in the room suddenly looking at me? Can they hear my thoughts?"

It's like they're eagerly waiting for me to say something creative and pioneering, a bit left field, waiting for me to suggest something to do or try.

The tall Doctor continues "It's your decision now as to whether we turn the ventilator off for your Dad?"

Have you ever been in a situation where you've had to make a choice, that you really don't want to make?

I never thought I'd be in a situation where I'd have to make this kind of choice. In contrast to the voices in my head, the confusion, the questions – Why? How? ...the room has come to a standstill, it's like time has stopped.

Looking around for inspiration...it's like I can see an image of a familiar cupboard door. It looks like the beautifully painted, green panelled 'Monica Geller door' (the one in the TV show Friends, where everything is stuffed, squeezed and balanced into the little space, locked away so that the world outside the cupboard looks organised, tidy and calm).

I can see the lock of the cupboard door, that has been holding it closed, it's unlocked and the door cracked slightly open...

...and it's as if suddenly, I can see the contents spilling out – I realise that I could call this the '**M.G. Cupboard**' not **M**onica **G**eller but the '**M**emories **G**ained **Cupboard'**.

1. **Out pops a bag marked "16 Years Old Choice - Thursday 4th Jan 1996"**

Dr Hamilton, a very welcoming and smiley man, with round spectacles and quite a jolly sized man. A bit like Santa Claus, only with dark and grey speckled short hair and beard. Dr Hamilton felt my tummy area.

"Janine! You need to get yourself straight over to A&E today. I can feel a large mass in your stomach and I want you to get this seen to today."

I can see me sitting in the hospital examination room, looking petrified with fear, at all the information, questions and choices being given to me. Alongside feeling the type of pain, I recall it as being like someone giving you a Chinese burn, at the same time as being intermittently stabbed with something sharp and then twisting it. Only this was happening on the inside of my tummy.

"Janine, you have a 2-pint size twisted endometriotic cyst, that has weaved between and stuck itself to your internal organs. The risk in not having surgery is the cyst may burst and you risk your life, or we operate straight away before it bursts and we will have to take the ovary too. Which will impact your ability in having children and leave you needing to be on medication, for the rest of your life."

I recall thinking "Wow, this feels like a no-win situation."
Pushing this memory back into the '**M.G. Cupboard'** another memory comes tumbling out.

2. **A new bag marked "18 Years Old Choice - Tuesday 10th February 1998"**

My mum, the morning of her birthday, has received the news that her mum, my nan has suddenly passed from a stroke. Triggering my mum to struggle with her own mental wellbeing, again, with the all-consuming grief of loss.

The choice made to support my mum and what she needed, left me overnight going from sleeping in my bed in the family home, to homeless. With no savings, sleeping on another's sofa, with my personal belongings in carrier bags and no place even my possessions can call home.

Quick, push this one back into the '**M.G. Cupboard**'…"oh no! there is another one falling out".

3. A box marked "19 Years Old Choice – Tuesday 4th August 1998"

I'm sitting on the hospital bed, waiting to go into surgery again. Here's the thing, this time it's for something else. I found a breast lump and I am waiting to go in to have it removed and sent for biopsy. I'm thinking, "Did I make the right choice on medication at 16 for my endometriosis? It was a risk!"

"This isn't the time Janine!", I say to myself. I push everything back into the imaginary space, squeezing against all the memories of choices and lock the door. I don't want to deal with these memories right now.

Back in the room, I look to see my mum, my sister and the tall Doctor still sitting in the small box room with me. Still frozen in time and motion, all eyes still on me, waiting for me to make a choice… if I make the choice to turn the ventilator off, never will my Dad walk me down the aisle, never see my sister's children and playing

horsey ride with him on his hands and knees around the lounge, playing badminton, playing board games, teaching them to fix cars, do D.I.Y, showing them how to prune roses and mow the lawn, letting them run under the sprinkler…you know, all the fun and happy things a Grandad does. This is my invincible Dad, who is as tough as an Ox and he always said…. "I'm living till 100". This is my Dad, who also throughout my childhood, teenage and early adulthood, reinforced in me that "there is no such word as CAN'T, you've ALWAYS got a choice".

4. A box marked "The Biggest Choice – Monday 7th January 2002"

As I nod to my mum, I realise that I'm making the choice. The truth is Dad isn't going to be able to do any of the plans, even if the ventilator stays on.

Have you ever had a time in your life, where it doesn't matter what the choice is, you feel like there is no choice?

That's exactly how I felt on this day.

I'd love to tell you that despite having to make this choice, that my life after not long turning 22 was easy. I'd love to tell you that's what happened…but actually, the devastation wasn't just for me. It was for my sister that found her long-term relationship end and being there, seeing the heart-breaking pain she was in…

…I put this in the cupboard.

My mum, who understandably found it increasingly difficult to cope with the situation, in fact, at one point we ended up sofa buddies.

Nowhere to call home…

…I put in the cupboard.

I'd love to tell you that after this choice, I started to build my life up, that slowly and surely everything started to get back to normal… but how could it? The truth is, what started to happen, is I just started to add even more things into that '**Memory Gathering Cupboard**' of mine.

Not only did I try to hide the contents and forget about them, I even hung 'the picture of guilt' over the door, so I couldn't even see the cupboard itself. And I used every distraction to forget all about the choices I'd made. There was distracting with work, I became successful and a workaholic. Looking in on me, my typical working week of 70-80 hours, commuting early hours of the day, late hours of the night. Even if I couldn't see the cupboard, it was still a memory in the making…in the cupboard, it went.

The familiar journeys on the motorways, the train stations, the many overnights in familiar hotels, trying to get away from it all. In the cupboard, it went.

Distracting with alcohol, G&T at the bar after work every single night and not just one. In the cupboard, it went.

Always trying to be the strong one. Pretending to be the strong one. Any fears went in the cupboard.

Have you ever heard the saying, that sometimes people come into your life so you can help them and sometimes it's so they can help you?

The help that I had, came in the form of one woman I met in America. I remember seeing from one of my online social media friends of a few years, a number of posts about a lady in America that had been doing some great mentoring and coaching in people's businesses and life. The posts caught my interest, as it was about how to forgive yourself and move on. I've got to be honest, I didn't know how to do that on my own. I didn't know how to open my '**M.G. Cupboard**' and look at all that was in there on my own.

It's May 2013. I'm hopping onto a plane over to America, to a large conference room in Pittsburgh, to meet with the women who helped me, called Dani. I remember meeting Dani in person. She has beautiful long blonde hair down to her waist, with an eye capturing bead of multi-tone grey pearls around her neck. To look at her, she reminds me of the late Caroline Flack, only with the American glow and super straight white teeth. Dani says something that changes how I look at my locked '**M.G. Cupboard**' and 'the picture of guilt' that hangs over it. She says "forgiveness is a choice. Choose to forgive yourself and then you can truly move on. You can choose to forgive yourself every day because you are human, flawed and most of all worthy of love. Learn from it and move on. Every day is another chance to start over".

These words stay with me over the next 3 days that I spend with Dani and keep repeating in my head. On the last day, Dani reminds me again of these words "forgiveness is a choice. Choose to forgive yourself and then you can truly move on. You can choose to forgive yourself every day because you are human, flawed and most of all worthy of love. Learn from it and move on. Every day is another chance to start over". I find Dani and these words breaking through the hinges of my '**M.G. Cupboard**' door,

sending 'the picture of guilt' I had hung over it flying. All the memories, choices I had pushed into and locked away in the cupboard, came tumbling out.

Everything was there for me to see…but here's the key, I am no longer on my own. I reached out for help and I'm now reprogramming my mindset in a guided way. See I discovered that our minds are like super-fast computers, with lots of programs we add in and we update to be customised to us. What we don't have is the anti-virus software that does the scanning, the checking to make sure that when we are customising our minds computer programs, that we don't download a virus that puts an always on screensaver over our operating files, and keeps them locked away ultimately stopping us, blocking us from accessing and doing what we need and dream to do.

I returned to America in November 2013, committing to looking at everything that tumbled out of my cupboard and reprogramming my mindset to include the anti-virus software. I've built myself a new routine into my daily life, I call it 'The M.I.N.D. Sweep Method' which is my uniquely designed, daily anti-virus scan of the cupboard, that really looks, sees, learns from and appreciates the choices I make. Making the choice, my choice, to be one of forgiveness of myself, learning from it and moving on, instead of locking it away in the cupboard and hanging the picture of guilt back over it.

Because here's what I believe…the choices we make in life shape us.

I'm forever grateful for the choices that I've made.
I'm forever grateful that I reached out for help.

I'm also forever grateful for the someone that came into my life, to help me, from my reaching out. With the help of someone else, I was able to open the cupboard door.

This is important. I also believe what set me free on my journey to forgiving myself, for the hardest choice of my life I took on Monday 7th June 2002…is I stopped pretending to be the strong one all the time and I reached out for help to look behind that locked cupboard door, with 'the picture of guilt' hung over it. The someone who came into my life, changed my perspective on what I was doing over the years and helped me to see why I didn't need to have an '**M.G. Cupboard**' and a 'picture of guilt' hung over it.

So many people, like me and like I did, try to pretend that their life external looks like the beautifully painted, green panelled '**M.G. Cupboard**' door. So many people try to pretend that their life's just so perfect.

But what's in your '**M.G. Cupboard**'?

Because here's the thing. Mental Health England report that 1 in 4 people are experiencing mental health issues each year and 75% of mental illness starts before the age of 18. What are the reasons 75% of mental illness starts before the age of 18? Well at the core of some of these reasons are environmental causes, such as, social stresses, created by activities like scrolling through those social media posts that appear to be oh so perfect, with lots of followers, lots of likes, lots of comments that create the feeling of comparison, makes you question and measure your worth and your value.

Other causes that contribute to this are isolation, substances abuse, pressure to perform well academically or in work, emotional

sexual or physical abuse, death of a parent or sibling, disruption in the home environment.

Here are some of the examples of what goes into the '**M.G. Cupboard**'. The rise in mental health issues, is reported by Mental Health England, to result in 72 million lost working days and costing £34.9 billion each year.

Would you agree with me…as a young child, a young adult, being the 1 in 4, is not what we dream our future will be?

And would you agree with me, that being the 1 in 4, is not what we set out to or want to create as our legacy?

However, my journey, my '**M.G. Cupboard**' with the 'picture of guilt' hung over it, shined a light on how you might not be 1 in 4 today and how easy it is tomorrow if, for example, you lose someone like I lost my Dad, that this can send you into despair.

See the truth is, it shouldn't be embarrassing, it shouldn't be seen as weak or that you are a lesser person to show your vulnerability, your authenticity, to reach out for help. In fact, to reach out for help, shows immense courage and emotional intelligence in recognising that we, humans, are not built to do it all alone.

Would you agree with me, that perhaps, it is time to take a reflective approach to the way we set ourselves, our children up for success? What we define as success?

Because, here's what I want you to know and remember…
…the truth is in life; is we do have a choice.

I'll say this again…
…the truth is in life; is we do have a choice.

I'm really pleased that all those choices have shaped me to be who I am today. All those choices have led me on a journey where I chose to come back and re-plan, re-design my life, like an architect would a house, just **without** the '**M.G. Cupboard**'.

Where am I now? Well, today you'll find me in my dream family home, with my dream fiancé, my beautiful two dogs and on an exciting new journey of making our scientific miracle family together.

And I love nothing more, having found my "purpose" in life, working with my clients to serve, create and inspire others to be their best A.U.T.H.E.N.T.I.C. versions of themselves and influence positive change in both the lives of others and their businesses. As such I have made it my mission to inspire and influence the lives of a million people and more globally.

Because this is important, even when it feels like a deep dark tunnel that you are in, there's always light at the end of the tunnel, there's always choices to be made…

…and here's the thing, there are always people to help you with those choices.

And, here's what I want you to know and remember…like the cupboard, unless they know about the cupboard, they just think you're ok and they are oblivious to what they can do to help you.

"Today I choose to live by choice."

Author: Janine Dunn

A quirky fact about me: I am a qualified Italian Polished Plasterer and like using my creative side to design and create new, luxury and unique marble and wall décor effects.

What I do now: Janine is an Entrepreneur, Motivational Speaker, Author, Business Mentor and Mindset Motivator, Agile & Digital Transformation Expert, Non-Executive Director.

Having found her 'purpose' in life to serve, to create, inspire and guide others to successfully navigate their way to become the best a.u.t.h.e.n.t.i.c.™ version of themselves and influence positive change in both the lives of others and their business.

Janine draws from her own successful navigation through a number of significant and life changing traumas, both personally and within her family network, such as finding herself from the family home at 18, the impact of Alzheimer's personally and to her family, the heart-breaking impact of cancer, disentangling diversity and inclusion.

As a result of successfully navigating her way to the brighter side of life. Janine has uniquely designed her tried and tested Master Your Motivational Mindset™ Masterclass, to guide and inspire a million people and more globally, to successfully navigate their way to become the best a.u.t.h.e.n.t.i.c.™ version of themselves.

Janine also combines over 20 years in successfully leading innovative, pioneering business and digital transformation projects and implementation. To now guide and teach other entrepreneurs and small businesses what to do, step-by-step, through her uniquely designed The Passport to Profit and Prosperity™ Programme, to make the changes that will lead you in both your

life and business to mine the nuggets of opportunity to pivot to Profit and prosperity, create resilience, especially in the digital age and much more.

How to connect to me:

www.janinedunn.com

support@janinedunn.com

I have a message just for you!
Scan me with your camera or QR app

“48 Hours”

Aly Jones

I don’t remember anything about that day, or leading up to that fateful event…
I don’t remember the conversations I had or what I wore…
Or how I got there?
Or even where ‘there’ was?

None of that mattered anyway ...

But I remember those words “48 hours”!

I remember feeling a sudden cold emptiness rush through my body.
I remember all sounds dissipating into distant echoes.
I remember feeling like my body had left the room.
Like all gravity didn’t exist and I was simply going to float away.

Nothing else - right there and then - mattered ... Except for those words “48 hours”.

48 hours...
That was the length of time I was given to empty my beautiful four bedroom house of its entire contents.
That was how long I had to walk away from my forever home that I’d just remortgaged to invest in upgrades and business dreams.
That was how long I had to give up all the hard work I’d done over the years to purchase my four bedroom house.
That was how long I had to relinquish my children’s inheritance!
That was how long it took to destroy my legacy!
That was how long it took for me, my husband and four very young children to become homeless!

48 hours" was how long it took to begin the next cycle of my life, one of the toughest in my life!

The story that led to this life changing word "48 Hours", actually began two years before, the beginning of July 2005.

My husband and I had been refurbishing our house, and we were really excited as we were in the process of starting our own business.

We had re-mortgaged our beautiful four bedroom semi detached house with en-suite and views overlooking the nature park and lake, so that we could make an offer on a suitable property we were about to invest in, for our new registered Care Home business we were about to start.

Everything was in place and coming together perfectly. We had the property checked by a Government Regulator for its suitability as a care home, and with plans for remodelling in place, we had been given the green light. We also had an investor interested too, and all the paperwork was ready and in place, with the deposit in the bank.

We were so excited! We had left nothing to chance. But ... we didn't factor in fate dealing us a joker!

We knew it was going to be a fabulous care home which we envisaged being open for business towards the end of the year, once all the interior had been refurbished and adapted.

It was the beginning of July 2005 at this point, and I was heavily pregnant in my sixth pregnancy and we were excited and hoping for a healthy 4th child.

Everything was going perfectly well...

...maybe in hindsight, too well.

My husband at the time was in a senior role within a care establishment and was well respected as he was good at his job. I was a week away from my due date and excited. Things were all finished with the refurbishments on our own house too. My husband had just taken 2 weeks off so we could work on getting our business started before the baby arrived. It was almost there.

On the Monday after having two weeks annual leave off, my husband returned to work. Later that day everything in our world changed forever!

Sadly, one of the service users within the care home died. As awful and traumatic as that was for everyone living and working within the home, it was devastating for my husband as he had been the one working closely with him when it happened and also the one who had found him dead and had tried to resuscitate him. What my husband didn't realise, whilst he was on his two week annual leave, the care plan for this service user had been changed due to the Service User's increasing seizures. But nobody - including Management had thought it necessary to inform my husband that morning on his return to work, either in the initial handover or in the message book, or the care plan front update page.

Initially, the company were behind him, offering support and counselling, knowing that he had done nothing wrong as my husband was very experienced in his role and had always carried out his duties diligently. Things started to change, and support dissipated when the company realised how serious the matter was when the Crown Prosecution Service got involved.

My husband was utterly shocked, distraught and devastated as well as grieving for the loss of someone he cared for. He didn't sleep and his usual evening drinking turned into all day drinking.

Initially, the company had allowed him to return to work for a further few days after the event, before realising it was in all best interests for him to be suspended on full pay. Before his suspension, my husband's sixth sense kicked in. He collected as much information as he could, making copies of rota's dating back several months, copies of specific parts of care plans and folders of other information that his sixth sense was telling him that he just might need! He knew it would become the ammunition for the fight ahead and for what was about to happen ...

...it didn't matter about what ammunition we had though. It was clear that the Company had already made up their mind before my husbands disciplinary that they were going to cover their own backs and sack my husband. That much was clear!

During all this chaos, angst, grief and turmoil, and just a week after the terrible incident...my daughter was born. We had a water birth planned and against the odds it went well. Well at least for a day we were happy. We had escaped our nightmare for a short while as we watched our daughter being born. We held her, grateful she was the perfection we needed in the imperfect world we were experiencing.

For a short while, we were at peace.

We left the hospital later that day with our beautiful new family addition and returned home to what was going to be our life of grief and strife for the next few years. At this point, I was not employed, as childcare would have been too expensive! I had a seven year

old girl, a thirty six month hyper toddler boy, a seventeen month daughter that was lactose intolerant. And now, a new born! To say I was too busy to work was an understatement! My husband was now so caught up with his own drama, he barely noticed the kids, let alone our newest beautiful addition.

During those first months, post that fateful event, he was too pre-occupied to feed them, change nappies, bathe them, read stories or put them to bed. He occasionally helped to make a bottle when I asked as this took little effort or thought or time away from the all consuming pending court cases. He was busy being investigated by Crown Prosecution Service (CPS), the Care Quality Commission (CQC) and attending company disciplinaries. He was immediately placed onto a list called Prevention Of Vulnerable Adults (POVA), preventing him from further work within care – treated guilty before innocence. Being put on this list meant my husband wasn't able to work in care again. This was a terrible blow and felt like another nail in the coffin. Not only did he feel bad enough about what happened, but now our dreams of running our own business were down the drain too. We were devastated!

The CPS completed their investigation and deemed that there had been no criminal act involved in the death of the service user and that no proceedings would be taken against my husband.

CQC (the regulating government body that overlooks all care providers) also looked into the matter and interviewed staff, service users, management and went through care plans. The outcome was that my husband be taken off the POVA list, and the company to follow all procedures whilst investigating all the actions that were taken before, during and after the event.

For the next two years, my big glass dining table became a desk of paperwork, notes and files as we built a case to take to the

Tribunal Court. In an ideal world and a fair world, we had a great case. We would easily have been able to prove in so many, different ways, that the company was at fault and were blatantly lying with facts. But life isn't fair is it, especially when you haven't got deep pockets?

Taking them to standard courts would have cost hundreds of thousands. We knew at this point with no job and me not working, as I had just recently given birth to my fourth child, that our savings wouldn't last long. Taking them to court ourselves, wasn't an option. The Detective from the CPS was very understanding once my husband was cleared, and could see what the company were doing. However, it wasn't a criminal offence, it was a civil offence for the courts to look into.

The only option we had, was to take the Company to a Tribunal for Unfair Dismissal!

We now had a huge mortgage, a new baby, no jobs and no other income! The refurbishment that we had just done on our own house had come from remortgaging, from the pot of money and savings that we were initially going to start our own business with before all this happened. The mortgage payments were now very high. We had calculated this cost as being affordable with our new business we had planned .... however, we hadn't accounted for no income at all! The pot of money for our business would now need to be used for keeping a roof over our heads…

…we were offered no help!

We had no family we could turn to financially.
We were not entitled to any benefits to help with our mortgage.
We felt helpless.

We felt devastated.
We felt angry.
We wanted to take my husbands company who had lied all the way through from the disciplinary and the investigation, to the CPS and CQC.

We wanted justice for the mis-treatment of my husband. There wasn't a way we could see forward to get the company to accept responsibility for their conduct, and the ultimate damage and devastation my husbands company caused to our family and future.

It wasn't fair!

So, the only option we had was to use the CAB (Citizens Advice Bureau) free legal services for an Unfair Dismissal Case. Two years it took. It was a long, hard two years. We won! But we won nothing!

In the time it took of almost 2 years to win our case, our savings had well and truly run out. They had lasted about a year. We eventually got help with some benefits to help support the children, tax credits, and a small grant for baby equipment and council tax benefits, but they couldn't help with our mortgage.

By Spring 2007 we were in Court, again…fighting for our house.

I still naively thought the judge would understand and take pity on us. But it seemed he took more pity on the bank we owed our mortgage to.

"48 hours" …. they were the dreaded words I will never forget!

We were officially homeless!!

My furniture and important belongings were placed in a friend's garage, whilst everything else we gave away or binned.

I remember the day I left my home, as I stepped out of my front door for the last time and walked past the two Court sent bailiffs with bolt cutters and padlocks in their hands. I don't remember their faces, just their dark clothes as I walked past them. My head hung in shame, with embarrassment and grief. I didn't imagine things getting worse, but they did!

A month later, whilst living in a hostel, all my belongings I had stored in the friend's garage were ruined from unprecedented monumental flooding in the area. The worst ever seen. And just like that, most of our stuff was gone too! After 2 years of enduring our struggle and fight, then this! I felt we had lost everything over again!

For six months we endured living in a hostel that we shared with numerous varieties of bugs, dirt, mould and rats.

I still felt shame and embarrassment.
I also felt like a failure too!
I believed I was a laughing stock to my friends, my family, the hot topic of gossip in my town – "it's not difficult to keep up with the Jones' now!"
I felt like I was failing my family, my kids.
I felt like I was in a fish bowl, with nowhere to hide and all my failures on show as I swam round and round in the same circle.
I thought I was the worlds worst parent.
I simply wanted to curl up in a ball…
…but my kids needed me!

My younger three kids took it all in their stride, as they were too young to understand what was going on. I made a conscious effort

at all times to keep it that way and stay happy around them. My eldest was 10 and it was harder for her. There was a park next to the hostel and kids called her names and swore at her through the hostel fence – “gypo”, “loser”, “dirty scum”, “poor”, “thick-o”. I cried for her.

I didn't think I would ever recover or feel good again.

But I did.
We all did.
We all made it... against all the odds!

And by October 2007 we finally got allocated our own house! It took a while to adjust to being in social housing, as it was something I had never experienced, having never grown up in social housing. However, I was so grateful to have a house after being in a hostel. I was absolutely over the moon! Our very own home again.

But...
I needed to mend the hurt, accept the defeat, and mourn the losses.
I needed to grieve as well as make our new house a home.
I needed to allow myself to be angry.
I needed to stop feeling guilty.
I needed to stop feeling a failure.
I also knew, that my family needed me more than ever to make us a 'normal' family again.

And so I did all of the above.

Sometimes I randomly cried, sometimes I laughed, sometimes I shouted, sometimes I smiled and sometimes I gazed off into the distance and just 'processed' it all.

It took time.
It took allowing me to enjoy myself again.
It took allowing me to feel everything at times.
It took allowing me to feel nothing at times.
It took allowing me to feel pain at times.
It took allowing me to feel grief at times.
It took allowing me to feel lost at times.
It took allowing me to just accept at times.
It took allowing me to just allow…

…slowly but surely, life started to normalise itself again .... at least for a while anyway.

Although I went on to experience further losses over the next year or two following this experience, in hindsight I realise it was one of the catalysts I needed to propel me onto my chosen life path.

I took to researching everything I could on the meaning of life and why we are here and what it all means. This was also the time when I really started on my spiritual journey of growth and self development.

In my personal journey of research and growth, I realised something special...

…we are not Physical Beings trying to achieve a spiritual life. We are Spiritual Beings already, here to live through physical experiences and emotions.

We are meant to experience a myriad of many things, feel a myriad of emotions. It is part of our learning and growth. It is what gives us wisdom, humility and compassion through empathy…if we allow it. When I look back today, I do so only with gratitude and

love for my experiences. My emotions as well as my losses, as hard as they were, have made me who I am today.

“48 hours” will always stay with me.

Except now I see it as the start of my life’s revolution rather than destruction.

Author: Aly Jones

A quirky fact about me: Aly grew up in the Middle East, returning to London when she was 13.

What I do now: Aly is passionate about positively inspiring audiences as an Impact Speaker and Empowerment Coach. Aly is very creative and loves to keep busy and is currently designing a stationary range. She is also a Project Director and Board Member, Networking Area Director for London and a Co Director for a New Holistic Retreats & Products Company.

Aly's own experiences and self-development journey over the years has allowed her to progress successfully as a business, within the Self-Development arena, particularly with her talks and workshops.

She is always developing herself through study, meditation, coaching and attending events and talks herself, she loves to learn new concepts and is always studying new courses and programmes to enhance her skills and knowledge.

Before turning her dream into reality and founding YBU Coaching, Aly would describe her life as having many steep but interesting learning curves, experiencing many personal adversities and challenges. She realised everything has a purpose including her own life, so decided to live to her higher purpose and turn her skills and experiences into becoming a Public Speaker to share her personal story of triumph over adversity.

Aly's vision is to positively impact and 'awaken' their inner super powers, reaching as many people globally as possible, through her talks, events, writing and collaboration projects.

Aly's talks inspire audiences and impact through her audiences in topics including Perception, Mental Health, Leadership, Authenticity, Resilience and Universal Laws.

How to connect with me:

 https://www.facebook.com/alyj3

 https://www.facebook.com/ybu.coaching

 @alyjones111

 www.linkedin.com/in/aly-jones-3972a2136/

 @YBUcoaching

www.ybucoaching.com

 www.ybu_coaching@outlook.com

I have a message just for you!
Scan me with your camera or QR app

Writing a New Chapter in Your Book Called 'Life'

Michelle Watson

As she sits at her glass desk, in the tiny but very comfy eye-catching turquoise blue and white office, located in her back garden, she gazes out the window located in front of her, which gives a full view to the back of her house. There is the refreshing smell of greenery as the sun streams in, and she starts to reflect on her journey.

"How did I get here?" The success, despite the many hurdles running through her mind, like pop up images on a big cinema screen, it had not been an easy ride that took her to this moment. The trophies, pictures, her books, and those of clients sitting on the shelves in the unit behind her, gives a brief glimpse into what she has been able to accomplish. A deep feeling of gratitude as a tear began to roll down her right cheek, looking at the house in front of her and remembering the day a bailiff stood outside the door of her house where she once lived, trying to get in to take away the few possessions both her and the two beautiful children she had at the time, had left.

"How did I get from there, to this? The question kept coming back to her in such a profound way, the only answer she could come up with was God, hard work and belief. If you were there in ear shot as she asked this question aloud, I am sure that you would have a few questions of your own to ask, where is there? Where was she coming from? What were some of the things she went through?

You see, now she is Michelle Watson, a Bestselling Author, Business Book Mentor & Publisher, Business Accelerator Coach, Multi-award Winning Speaker, Co-Pastor and the Founder of Breakfree Forever Consultancy Ltd. She is also the proud mother of three beautiful children and a wife to one of the best men in the world. However, despite the many accolades that I now have there is a story and journey behind it all, things did not come about easily and maybe as you are reading this right now, you can relate.

For a long time, I was lost, unsure of where my life would be and the purpose of me being here on this earth. For some that know me but do not know my story they may be thinking 'really?'

Well join me in the year 2005 and here you see me in a very challenging situation, I am just coming in from a night of dinner and cinema with my friends, with a banging headache and my heart pounding so hard it feels as though my chest is about to burst, and if you are wondering, no my headache is not from drinking. I am standing with my back against the locked door in my small magnolia painted bathroom. The white porcelain bath to my right, the toilet to the front on my left and the face basin immediately in front of me below a window I believe is too massive for a bathroom, the distinct smell of bleach playing havoc on my nostrils, but I could never clean my bathroom without a lot of bleach, I just wish it could help to clean all the muck that is in my life right now.

'Oh no is that him?' I jumped as I heard a sound and crouched sideways to put my ears close up to the door. I know he's not gone and is still out there waiting for me to come out. Why am I here again? Over and over I tell myself no more – it is not going to happen again, but somehow, I still end up finding myself in the same or worse position. Nicky keeps telling me, but I never listen, "Michelle you don't see that he is going to kill you, are you going to remain like this forever?" "You refuse to tell your family and all you

do is get up and write in journals as if you can write it all away."

Nicky is a close friend of mine; you know the ones that tell it like it is with her hint of Jamaican accent. She just does not understand, I cannot just leave and become a divorcee in my early twenties. How can someone that once looked at you with so much love and compassion now look at you with such hate? How can the hands that once made you tingle with life, now made you feel pain? How could the smile that once made you melt, now just curdled your blood and the words that made your heart skip a beat now changed to so much filth that you felt like the scum of the earth. Dr. Jekyll and Mr. Hyde, you know the character with two personalities and to be going through this with him for five years has slowly destroyed me.

The shame of telling my family is too much, to tell anyone would be too much. Nicky only knew because she had seen the marks and heard the sounds. All I wanted was one night out with my friends, I had just been told that I had a tumour behind my left ear, resting on my nerve and there was a 99% chance that the left side of my face would be paralysed after the operation, and I just wanted to be with my friends, something that I had also been deprived of and as you can guess, he was not happy about that. So here I am with my head spinning like a butterfly and my bruises stinging like a Bee as if I had just gone through a few rounds in the ring with the great Muhammad Ali.

Oh no the kids! I must get out; I cannot let him take the kids. Have you ever had to make a decision - a very big decision? Well that night I decided not to just face whatever was coming to me by stepping out of the bathroom, but I also stepped out of the marriage. I would love to tell you that it was easy, but it was not as I found it hard to tell my family as I felt ashamed and spent most days staying at my friend's house.

However, have you ever played the board game Snakes and Ladders? You've shaken your dice and got the biggest numbers, two sixes and you happily move up your spaces, and oh boy you are excited, because you end up also getting a bonus to climb higher by going up the ladder, only to land on the mouth of a snake which takes you all the way back down to his tail, at the very beginning of the board? Have you ever felt like that, as if you are running through hoops but getting nowhere?

Well 4 months later you would see me stepping into yet another small room. Brilliant white painted walls, dark brown sofa to my right, a desk and chair to my left and a massive plant standing in the corner. There was a lovely smell of summer breeze and the room was brightly lit but somehow, I seemed to have darkness all around me. There he is tall dark and handsome, he could be a basketball player, apart from the glasses pitched on his nose that made him look a bit like a nerd. Hello Michelle, do come in and take a seat, is it alright for me to call you Michelle? With his bright yet soft spoken voice. "Yes" I replied hardly being able to open my mouth. "I prefer to stand if that's okay" "Yes Michelle, whatever makes you comfortable, so I have gone through your notes and forms you have filled, but can I hear from you what really brings you here today".

My hands began to shake and the erratic, cracked voice that began to speak sounded nothing like me. "I feel like I am going mad and I know they think I am going mad, but I know he is following me." "Michelle who is following you?" "My ex he is following me where ever I go, I will go to the store and he's there, I leave my house to go to work and when I returned all my clothes was missing from the closet, another time it was my purse and passport. I go to my friend's house and all my four tyres gets slashed outside her house, that is not a coincidence. Every morning I get up my car has another key mark on it, I have gone to

my bed and woken up to find him standing over me. No one seems to be able to help, the police said that because he lived there his fingerprints would be all over the house anyway and unless they have proof, they cannot prevent him from coming to the house. I was too ashamed to tell my family all that is happening. I cannot eat, sleep or even take care of the children properly, I can't take it anymore, I just can't take it anymore! The tears flowing along with what little strength I had left.

"Michelle, it is ok, but is that the reason why you decided to try and attempt to kill yourself?"

"I just want the pain to stop, I know it was wrong. How could I do this to my beautiful children? Who would have been there for them, My beautiful Santana, who would be there when it's time for her prom or Rashaun my sweet boy, he has special needs you know, who would be there to help him? How could I do this, how could I do this? I just want it all to stop." "It will Michelle, it will, as you did the right thing by getting in touch, I always say to my clients that no one can answer a phone call that wasn't made, you have made the call and we are help to help you. You are stronger than you know, I read through your notes and realised that whilst dealing with all this you recently had an operation to have a tumour removed, I assume all went well?" I replied with a nod of the head. "Michelle it's not too late to turn your life around, with the right help you will be fine, you will be there to look after your children but in order to do that you have to first take care of you. I can see from your notes here that one of your favourite hobbies is writing, well guess what, you have the ability to re-write your history and turn things around, you just have to allow us to help you."

Re-write my history…..what did Nicky ask me again? Oh yes, do I think it is possible to write my life away? Here he is telling me that I have the ability to re-write my history.

Have you ever had a time in your life when you wished that your life was actually a physical book where you could go back and rip out the pages of the things in the past you did not like, or wasn't happy about, maybe that ex, or that costly mistake that you made? Unfortunately, that's not possible but I realised at that moment that I may not be able to rip out the pages, but that I could make a difference to my future, and so with the help of the councillor, my church and family you would have seen me stepping into my power.

You would have seen me on a spiritual journey whilst also working on myself through personal development. I started reading self-development books like Dale Carnegie, "How to win friends and Influence People," Robin Sharma, "The Saint, The Surfer and The CEO," Joyce Meyer, "Battlefield Of The Mind," and Willie Jolley, "A Setback is a Setup For A Comeback." I started to listen to powerful people like Les Brown, Lisa Nichols, Tony Robbins and Jim Rohn. You would have seen me on a spiritual journey as well as attending seminars, mastercoach, and the coaching academy to achieve my accreditation as a Life Coach. The Mpowerment Ltd where I learnt NLP (Neuro Linguistic Programming) and you would have seen me finding out who Michelle truly was. I then decided that I wanted to help people as well, just like how the councillor, my pastor and the personal development world had helped me, and so I signed up to a programme to write my story, so I could share it and help even if it was one reader that would read it.

Now, there were some people on the way, you know those people, the Naysayers, "So what qualifies you to write a book?" "Will anybody buy your book when they don't even know you?" "You went through depression and attempted suicide; how can you be qualified to write a book in order to help others – are you for real?" "So, you are JK Rowling now huh?" However, I decided that even if the book just helped me to get everything out there, then that

would be enough. Nevertheless, people were coming up to me, slowly but surely and saying, "Wow your story was amazing." "You need to share this story, it really helped and inspired me." This was all great, but I had used up the last of my savings to write the book, and now that I did, and I was inspiring others with my story, there was no money coming in, and the business that I had in mind seemed terribly far away.

At this point I had now used all my savings, wages and sold items to invest in personal development. My now new husband Allain thought I was mad, but I told myself that when I made my money back, I could always replace them. I had now learnt that I needed to get my message out to more people, not just one-on-one, not just one person reading my book, but that I could share the message of hope and help as many people who, just like me, got dealt a bad card, and that's why I decided to take action, because I wanted to help those who have been on that road, just like me, but the question was how?

The book, even though becoming a bestseller was not doing anything, I had started my business on the side as a Certified Life Coach but that was not moving. I was going from one mentorship programme to the next, attending the seminars, getting psyched up, return home and back to square one, as I had no idea what to do. It became frustrating as I kept meeting other authors like myself that had a book but then that was it, they were not known and I kept hearing the common story of how they spent all this money to write their book or start their business but then that was it.

I started to retrace my steps to what had brought me this far, what I had put in place that worked, remembering a statement I had heard from one of my mentors, I then decided at that moment to write down all the challenges I was currently facing and see how I

could solve it.

I then wrote my second book Rise Above and Believe, I wrote, edited, designed, the full works and published it in 90 days, this book was written based on the modules for my coaching programme. I decided to use it as a business tool and see how I could use it to drum up business. I sent a copy to Her Majesty the Queen and got a letter of Commendation, I did Media releases and started to get TV and Radio interviews, I was getting asked to speak at more events, and then I created my own events.

The first one being Women Be – a women empowerment and networking event, and with the experience and knowledge now gained I was able to create my business, having multiple streams of income.

I created a programme to help business owners and entrepreneurs write their business book, and use it as a marketing tool, as I successfully did it for myself. I began helping individuals that had ideas, but did not know how to turn it into a monetised business. I began to win numerous awards, Mentor Of The Year, multiple speaker awards, Performance Coach Of The Year, Empowerment Woman Of The Year, just to name a few. I have mentored and helped people, ranging from business owners to professional boxers and singers, and published numerous authors who have also become bestsellers and award winners, including my eight year old daughter Alisha. I am now truly fulfilling my purpose and leaving my mark on this earth, so those to come will know I was here.

As I sit here in my office and the memories come flooding through, I never ever dreamt I would have been able to pull myself from that dark place that I once was, there is still so much that I still have not shared with you, as the story would never end. The truth really is

that your story never ends, until you have left this earth. It does in some way continue. If a legacy is left for others to follow on from, that has always been one of my greatest desires.

I want to remind you though, that despite the fact that I am no longer where I used to be, does not mean that challenges no longer come, as I sit here writing my story my heart is in pain with the loss of my nan who was so dear to me, she was my mother from the age of three, she was my best friend. Only one of the many hurdles I have had to jump and I'm still jumping.

There are many that tend to paint the picture that their life is all perfume and roses, when behind there is a different story, because they want to remain 'professional' or be seen as 'flawless' in the public eye, so they make it seem like their life is smooth sailing and that they have everything under control. I do not believe in this, I believe strongly in being authentic and allowing your vulnerability to be seen, I am not saying to go out sympathy seeking but be open and real, this is what others will learn from.

I have always said I would never want a mentor who is telling me that they have never faced some sort of challenge or experience in life. My question is how will they then assist me during my difficult moments?

We all in life have difficult moments to go through, it just may differ from each other, and therefore we all have a story to tell. You may be saying 'but Michelle I have never gone through domestic abuse or attempted suicide,' this does not mean that your story is any less or not worth sharing.

I have learnt some valuable lessons on this journey, which I will share with you.

"Success does not define you but instead you define success." - Hazel Breen

You are the one that has the ability to determine your own success. Your success does not build you as the individual, but instead, who you are and become creates true success. You should also never let others define the measure of your success, no one will ever know your true strengths, to be honest even you do not recognise your own strengths until you have faced the test. Creating your own definition of being successful is what should guide and direct your life choices. Everyone's idea of what success is tends to differ, so therefore having your success gauged by someone else will not help you moving forward. You may not be where you desire to be as yet, but that does not mean it will not happen or be possible, keep your goals in sight, believe in yourself and don't settle for less than you deserve.

"You don't have to be great in order to start, but you do need to take a step in order to achieve your greatness" - Zig Ziglar

There is not one great person that started off that way, they had to persevere and overcome many difficult periods on their journey. We all must begin at the starting point, therefore stop telling yourself that you are not good or do not know enough. Take one step at a time and equip yourself with the resources you need as you go along. If you compare yourself to others you may get discouraged, therefore run your own race, and remember the race is not for the swift but the one that endures to the end.

"You might not be able to go back and rip out the pages of your past that you are not happy about but you do have the power to determine what will be written in the next Chapter of your book called life." - Michelle Watson

I believe that in life we all have a destiny and a purpose, the route to get to that destination is filled with many lessons (Challenges) to prepare you for when you arrive. I want you to stop right now and think about the people that you are either currently helping, or desire to help in the future, and you will realise that it is most likely something from your journey that has guided you to this WHY.

I cannot change what happened to me, but I made the decision that I was not going to let it dictate my future or legacy, I did not want to be remembered as a victim of domestic abuse, but instead as a survivor, a voice of influence. I was no longer going to allow my life to be determined by someone else, I want you to always remember this, the moment that you are living your life based on others, that moment you become a living dead.

I had stopped living and the only way I could change that was to stop living for the past, but instead for what I wanted my future to be. The choice is yours, you can choose to be governed by what you went through, and keep mulling over the pages of the past, or open your book to write a new chapter.

It is time to start believing, and living YOU, not the you that you want people people to see, but the you that smiles, the you that feels satisfied, fulfilled and happy about what you are doing.

It is time to share YOU with the world, you have gone through the dark moments, it is now time to be the light to help those coming behind so that they don't stumble, and if they do fall they can see the light to get up and begin to walk again.

The last lesson and words that I want to share with you is a quote I often say that has encouraged so many on their pathway.

***"A story not shared is a message not heard and a life not saved"* ~** Michelle Watson

Author: Michelle Watson

A quirky fact about me: I used to drive a train

What I do now: I am a book Mentor & Publisher, the founder of Breakfree Forever Consultancy, I serve Entrepreneurs, Speakers, Business Start-ups and individuals who want to share their story & expertise with the world to make an impact, create income, increase their business & leave a legacy behind.

How to connect with me:

https://www.facebook.com/breakfreeltd/

@iammichellewatson

www.linkedin.com/in/bookpublishing-businesscoach

@michellewatson@breakfreeltd

I have a message just for you!
Scan me with your camera or QR app

Who Am I?

Lisa King

Being a Public Speaker, Author, Mentor, TEDx Speaker and Clarity Trailblazer, I am living my dream life. I am at peace, I have an amazing life, I am looking forward to the future, I love being present and living in the moment, and I am at peace with my past.

If you would have asked me to write this chapter 6 years ago things would have been so different. Life had been a rollercoaster the previous 3 to 4 years. I had lost my partner, my best friend to suicide. I had self-destructed with drugs, drinking and making bad choices with who I spent time with, and I had a breakdown. Life had reached the point where I had choices to make.

The biggest choice was, do I want to go back to life as I knew it, or did I want to choose a life of Fulfilment, Joy and Inner Peace. Thankfully I chose the latter and the journey began, and what a journey it was, and continues to be.

My biggest challenge was to understand who I was without the masks, who I was without the coping mechanisms, who I was if my barriers were down. The truth was I didn't know, I had worn masks from such a young age, I had used so many coping mechanisms throughout my life, I really didn't know who I was without them. This time though I knew I had to find out. The pain of staying the same was much greater than the pain of changing.

Looking back I could see patterns, in relationships, with recurring illnesses, with business frustrations, it was clear to see. It was when I was in it, living it, that I was on the hamster wheel, on autopilot, that I couldn't see it. It took a tragedy and losing my best

friend to wake me up, to see where my life was heading.

To everyone else I was successful, had my own businesses, I was living life, having lots of fun, I had lots of friends, an amazing family life, I had it all. I thought so too.

It took Becky's death and my subsequent breakdown for me to step back, to look at what I really wanted, to find me, I use the word find, because I felt lost, so much had happened throughout my life.

I could go back to the old life easily, or I could face the biggest journey of my life, to find me, to uncover the Lisa underneath the masks, before the drink, drugs, lack of self-worth, the hamster wheel, and that is exactly what I did. I CHOSE ME.

I knew I had to focus on me, to go inwards, to look at who I was, what I loved to do, what brought me joy, what things do I lose track of time doing, and I needed to look inwards, and not focus externally for others to give me that.

I also knew I needed to focus on the things that were in my life, where I felt that I had to be someone else, like putting on an act, doing things I didn't really enjoy doing, going places to satisfy others rather than speaking up and saying no. The people-pleasing needed to stop, more on this later.

When you have been on autopilot for so long, over 30 years in my case, it took time, I needed to take one step at a time, it was so ingrained in me that I needed to learn, to understand which behaviour was me, being truly me, and what was my autopilot, my subconscious behaviour, that was having such a negative impact.

The most obvious place to start was with my childhood, and I could

write a whole book about that, as so much happened. I'll tell you the most significant parts and how they impacted me.

Growing up around Domestic Violence was tough, watching your mum be physically beaten, verbally abused, emotionally abused on a regular basis was horrendous. I heard it all, saw most of it and felt everything. Let me be really clear, my dad didn't hit us, the pain he dealt us was the broken promises, never being around, choosing everyone else over his family, disappearing for weeks on end with no word, there are so many more examples. How that impacted me was feelings of abandonment, feeling unloved and unlovable, feeling unworthy, I couldn't trust, and I felt like I wasn't good enough. I didn't understand the significance of these feelings until later in life.

This isn't about blaming my dad for everything, although I did that for many years, this is to show you an example of how a child's beliefs can impact them throughout their lives, in my case the negative beliefs I had formed, snowballed. Interesting fact though, I later found out that dad had also grown up around similar circumstances, in fact, my grandad was in prison for most of my dads' early years. Would it have been better for us if dad was away from us? Trust me, I used to ask myself this on many occasions.

As I look back, filled now with Self Compassion, Self Love, Self Respect and an Inner Peace I never dreamed possible, things could not have been further from the truth growing up. At 12, I was raped. It was by people I knew and trusted, looking back, this had such a significant impact on me, as this was the start of me shutting down, although I didn't actually realise that I was doing that until much later, 35 years later, as I had buried this incident so deep in my mind and just carried on, as if it never happened.

After the rape, alcohol entered my world and became a way of coping, as well as a way to have some control, or so I thought. The alcohol was to become my go-to throughout my life, regardless of whether I was celebrating, commiserating, stressed, happy, I no longer needed an excuse, the snowball was getting bigger and bigger. I also started shoplifting, that was the rebellious side of me coming out I think, and I was also starting to experiment with sniffers and things like that. The only reason I stopped shoplifting was because I knew how broken-hearted my mum would be if I got caught and ruined my future, and I didn't want to do that to her. There was no thought for the consequences to me, another sign of the lack of self-respect I had, it was always about others, not me.

Into my teenage years and the problem was I needed connection, I craved feeling wanted and that feeling of connection came from the wrong people. That's when the drinking, the lack of self respect and self love really spiralled, I had developed an unhealthy attachment to alcohol, some would say I was your typical teenager, they never knew the half of it. Even though I was a top sports student, Country Cross Country Champion, in the hockey and netball teams, athletics too, the alcohol was there, and on top of that, I had now started smoking too, and not just cigarettes.

School suffered, things at home were so intense, and to make it worse nobody knew, it was kept a secret, we were living two lives. When dad finally left when I was fifteen, I had mixed reactions, I was angry, I was heartbroken, my emotions were all over the place, and looking back it was the best thing for us, mum had had enough, she had been doing her absolute best to keep us together, working tirelessly, supporting us and being our only source of unconditional love and support. The following few years dad continued to break promises, putting everyone else first, until he then emigrated to Australia when I was 18.

So the foundations of my beliefs were well and truly set, the

snowball was getting bigger and bigger, life continued to be filled with fun, football, going out socialising, working hard and playing hard, and relationships that seemed to follow a certain pattern.

Understanding my past relationships, particularly relationships with partners was an eye-opener. The beliefs I held from a young child were centred around lack of trust, abandonment and vulnerability, (no wonder my relationships followed such a pattern). Vulnerability was not an option for me, so the minute anyone got close to me, and I felt vulnerable, or I felt like they may leave or that something had changed, I would leave the relationship immediately, with no warning, I'd just go, or I'd create an argument so I could leave, (I wonder where I learnt that skill). Looking back now I can see how mad that behaviour was, I truly knew no different, it was so ingrained in me.

The amazing thing now is that I am married to my gorgeous wife Penny, we have a fantastic relationship, and for the first time in a relationship I am me, the good, the bad and the damn right cheeky ☺, all of the time. No masks, no barriers, no coping mechanisms. She has supported me, loved me and been through the journey with me. Has it been perfect, no of course not, no relationship is perfect, I like to think of it as Perfekly Imperfect, just as we want it to be.

Now back to the masks. You may be thinking what do I mean by masks. For me, I wore many masks to cope with life. One of them and the one I wore for the longest time was my People Pleaser mask. This for me meant, lending money, even when I didn't have it, to the point that I almost lost my house. Buying rounds of drinks most of the time in social situations, I was constantly doing it, the money I spent was madness. Giving my time to help others, even if I was exhausted was a regular thing too, which meant I was too tired to do the things I wanted to do, and it needed to stop.

My people-pleasing, could be looked at in different ways, for me it came from feeling like I had to earn peoples love, I had to go above and beyond as I felt I wasn't enough so I had to be at their beck and call, to help them, regardless of the negative effect on me. This went on for many, many years, and led to my health deteriorating in many areas during this time.

I know you may be thinking, helping people is a good thing, it's a kind thing to do. I totally agree, I still help people, I'm very kind, I'm very giving. The difference now is that I do not do it at the detriment to my own mental, physical or emotional health. What good is it if I am giving people the rest of me, and not the best of me. There are also negative impacts on the people you are helping if you constantly sort their problems out for them.

Please understand I make the next comment with love.

By fixing people's problems you are actually, disempowering them from finding their own solutions, ask me how I know. I did it for many years, thinking I was helping, truly believing I was doing the right thing. It wasn't until I started to understand that I could still help, hold space, be their support, and guide them to do what I would have done, yet they do it for themselves. It makes them stronger it builds their confidence to be able to sort their own challenges out, and they still know you are there for them if they need you.

I truly believe we have all worn a People Pleaser mask at some point, in different ways, to different extents. The important thing to remember is that if you are constantly giving, and you are not taking the time to rest, to recharge and to give to yourself, your body is so out of balance. It is crucial to bring yourself back into alignment, receive from others too, trust me your body will reach a point where it says enough is enough, and potentially sickness,

Illness and burn out, will follow. After 3 burnouts and a breakdown, I have the t-shirt for this one.

I am often asked how did I make the changes, what exactly did I do. There were so many different things, and we are all unique so situations will vary, below are three of the changes I made that had the most positive impact.

Saying No

This created more time and energy for me to say yes to the things I wanted to do, with the people I wanted to spend time with. This does not mean that you will never again go to a certain place, or be with certain people, it just simply means that at times, you must choose you, your time and your energy. I truly believe those that matter won't mind and those that mind, don't matter.

Creating Boundaries

This was huge for me. If you have people or situations that you are not completely happy with, creating boundaries is crucial, not important, crucial. Yes, you may get some resistance, in fact, I'd be really surprised if you didn't, as people are used to you being or doing things in a certain way. Stick to your guns, they will get used to it, you must stay strong, maintain the boundaries because your health depends on it. If they are persistent with their negativity, then the right people will stay in your life and the right people will leave your life. That sounds harsh, but do you really want someone in your life that does not respect you or your boundaries?

Doing things that bring me joy

This was a lifesaver for me because I had more time as I had stopped saying yes to everything and everyone, I had created boundaries, I now had the time to do the things I loved, connecting with family and friends, spending time in nature, meditating, all the things I hadn't fully been present doing for a long time.

Making the changes that I have written in this chapter, not only reduced so many negative emotions, anger, frustration to name a few, it also increased my self-love, self-respect and self-worth and it continues to improve. There have been tears of joy, tears of sadness and many more in between along the way.

For me, understanding the coping mechanisms I had used from a young child, reframing events, having compassion for myself and forgiving myself and others were key. Please do not get me wrong, I can still get triggered, if that happens, I just need to recognise it and see where I am not being true to me, make the changes and get back on track. The key is to do this quickly, so you don't get back into bad habits and that negative autopilot.

And one of my proudest moments and the biggest Self Love exercise for me on the journey has been to stop drinking. This brings me so much joy to say. I am so very proud to say that I have not touched a drop of alcohol for (at the time this book has been published), for 2 years and 8 months. One of my biggest coping mechanisms has now gone. I no longer need it, want it, miss it, or rely on it.

If you ever feel like you want to make positive changes and you don't know where to start. Just start, before you talk yourself out of it. Take one step at a time, you can do it. Remember to reach out and ask for help if you need it, join groups where you can be around people that will inspire you, empower you and support you to make the change. You are Amazing and YOU CAN DO IT.

I would like to finish my chapter with one of my favourite quotes by Lao Tzu.

"The Journey of a Thousand Miles Begins with the First Step"

Author: Lisa King

A quirky fact about me: I love to change my hair style on a regular basis, from flat, to spiky, to half and half, however the mood takes me ☺

What I do now: Lisa is a Motivational Speaker, International Best Selling Author, TEDx Speaker, Mentor and Clarity Trailblazer.

Lisa's passion is to empower and inspire people to reach their highest potential, to fulfil their brilliance and live life on their terms. Creating the change they want to see in their lives, by being the truest version of themselves, inspiring others around them to do the same. Lisa runs her own CFG events and workshops, creates online courses, speaks in schools empowering our future generations. She has also created her membership, Clarity, Focus and Growth Collective and this is where this book originated. An idea from years ago, waiting for the right people to join her to share their stories. And here it is, the first of many CFG books and many more exciting projects.

You can watch Lisa's TEDx talk here:
www.youtube.com/watch?v=Pm3BPQxWTo8

How to connect with me:

https://www.facebook.com/lisaking49

lisa@clarityfocusandgrowth.com

I have a message just for you!
Scan me with your camera or QR app

Megan's Choice and Legacy

Jenny Copeland

On the 17th January 1981 my beautiful, fun, joyful mother completed her suicide by drowning. Three months before, I had sat in a doctor's surgery and the doctor said to me and my father "Take your mum home. Make sure she takes her tablets. Tell her you love her every day. That's all we can do for her." I don't think I ever felt guilty about my mother's death. However I did often wonder why my love wasn't enough to keep her alive?

Fast forward 40 years and once again I found myself in the doctors consulting room having much the same conversation, however this time we were talking about my beautiful, fun, joyful daughter Megan. This time it was after 7 years of revolving door emergencies, suicide attempts, inpatient sessions and wonderful, glorious, precious periods of "normality" and peace.

On the 16th July 1999, Rob, my husband, and I were blessed with the birth of our beautiful baby girl Megan. The pregnancy had been relatively uneventful, however at 36 weeks Megan decided to turn in the womb and corrected her breach position.

At 40 weeks there was no sign of Megan and I was left to grow my baby for a further three weeks. Finally, my waters broke but the labour did not progress. There was a strangeness to my contractions. It was as if the baby did not want to be born and was somehow retracting after each contraction.

A doctor was called and within minutes we were in theatre and Megan was delivered by caesarean section. She had managed to

entangle the cord around her neck and had been choking herself during her birthing journey in the birth canal. Megan didn't cry for three days and when she did make a noise it was a squeak. When she did finally find her vocal cords she squalled like a banshee.

I now recognise this as Megan's first trauma.

Over her short 20 years, she suffered many more. Undiagnosed medical issues. Undiagnosed mental illness. Rape. Rejection and finally a broken heart.

During the last 6 months of Megan's life, after a short inpatient stay which was preceded by a massive overdose, the same week, her daddy was having surgery for cancer, another trauma in her young life, Megan visited A&E three times. Each time she had ligature marks on her neck and each time she was free to leave with no therapeutic follow-up.

I arranged a meeting with her psychiatrist, a lovely helpful man, who explained there was little anybody could do for Megan and we should take her home and "tell her you love her."

On the 30th September 2019 barely 20 years old, Megan completed her suicide with a cord around her neck. Oh, the irony that she left this mortal coil in much the same way she entered it.

I once again, this time with Rob, was left with that same question "**Why wasn't our love enough keep her alive?"**

As a family, we had all worked hard to keep Megan alive. We had a tag system for monitoring her movements and she was rarely left alone. As a young adult, this was not sustainable and was certainly no way for her to live the rest of her life.

On July 16th 2020 the day we should have celebrated our daughters 21st birthday. We went to church and then we went to her grave. Due to her mental illness or dis-regulation, she will be "forever 20" due to her completed suicide. Our priest Father Willie Boyd led a small service and Rob shared the meaning of Megan's floral tribute.

I took the opportunity and spoke these words at her graveside.

"There are so many dum di dum poems that talk of love and above and perish and cherish.
You're too good for that.
You're worthy of Shakespeare and Keats. Dickens and Bronte.
Your life is a story that needs to be told and retold.
Analysed and learnt from.
Forensically dissected and explored under a microscope.

We are lucky that pretty much all of the photos we have of you are happy ones. The memories of the really difficult time's will fade and in time we will be left with an idealised version of your life.

Today it may help to just recall the trauma and pain you endured.
The crushing, desperate need to leave your skin.
The total inability to see or love yourself as clearly everyone else did.

We do this not to feel sorry for you or to somehow justify your final act but to seek to understand and respect that act.
And to stand here today with our hearts breaking and faces wet with tears to honour you.

Later after we dry our tears, we start a new way of honouring you through your charity Megan's Space.

We will be your voice.
We will be your balm.
We will be your legacy.

You, my love, will always be our brightest guiding star to light the path of our journey.

We will carry your light and, in your name,
in the name of love do you proud.
Happy birthday Megan sweetheart."

Megan's story is tragic by any stretch of the imagination, however, remember that 40 years ago I was told to take my mother home and love her as a treatment plan for her chronic depression and psychosis. 40 years later the advice is the same, as is the outcome, just the means different.

The true definition of madness is to keep doing the same thing expecting a different outcome. Clearly, we have a certain madness regarding our mental health services.

As mentioned, there is another irony that at much the same time as Megan had her major relapse in February '19 her father, Rob, had his cancer diagnosis confirmed.

He was told on a Friday afternoon he had cancer and was immediately transferred to the Beatson, one of Scotland's Cancer Centres of Excellence. He was given an appointment for the next Monday and on arrival, he was given a 16-week treatment and care plan that covered everything from dental to financial, radiotherapy, to speech and language, nutrition and emotional support. Today, a year later he is in remission. I thank the NHS for this.

By way of contrast, after Megan had been declared fit from a medical point of view and discharged from the hospital, she was admitted into a mental health unit. Although she was given a place of safety and care, she did not have the same intensive treatment plan and support as Rob, and no therapeutic interventions. Maybe none of this was required, however the stark difference between one care episode and another was baffling.

Additionally, Megan's regular A&E attendances with visible signs of extreme self-harm resulted in nothing. No detailed support and treatment plan and no therapeutic follow up.

I share this, not as an example of neglect, but as a contrast to the intensive investment in research and money available to the cancer service versus the mental health service. Underfunded, understaffed and overused.

So, when Megan died, we vowed to become activists in her name. Activists of love and equity for the young mentally unwell. We cooked up a concept and called it Megan's Space. We wanted young people to have a safe space to be heard and cared for. To have speedy access to therapy and to provide support and guidance to their families.

Our original target was a cheeky and ambitious £5k. We posted a Megan's Space JustGiving page on Facebook and bam, £5k in 5 hours! As of going to print we are nearer to £28k all told.

In many ways, it was good that we didn't fully appreciate what we were undertaking. Over the last 10 months, we have been working in the background helping people where we can.

We have received enquiries for assistance and have been able to either give advice, or refer young people quickly to other agencies

for support. We have already, I am sure, saved lives. But we are only getting started, there is so much we do not understand relating to the complex root causes of mental illness, however we do know that our young ones are enduring:

- Adulterated food chains,
- Electronic over stimulation,
- Relentless educational demands,
- Unrealistic images from social media, TV and films,
- Constant bombardment of advertising of shiny stuff!
- A lack of resources to research and educate regarding this list.

Megan was an intelligent, strong, independent child. Her first sentence was "me do it" and yet she succumbed to the myriad of traumas her young body was exposed to.

In the last 40 years, trillions of pounds and dollars have been spent researching cancer. It may surprise you to know that £124 million is currently invested in the UK on mental health research on average each year, that's £9 per person. Does this seem like a lot? By comparison, £612 million is spent on cancer research each year, which translates to £228 per person affected – or 25 times more per person.

Given that we now predict that 1 in two people will be affected by a mental health issue at some point in their life, it isn't enough, and it isn't equitable. We need to change the environment and the outcomes. Nobody else will do it. So... it's time to talk!

Megan pretty much wrote the manifesto for Megan's Space when at 17 she has already experienced first-hand the effects of underfunding. We are merely fulfilling her ambition; to make positive changes in mental health services for young people.

Megan will be “forever 20”. So no key of the door. No graduation ball. No wedding dress shopping or baby showers ... and no daughter to nag me to stay young and trendy when I go shopping. Rob will never get to walk his daughter down the aisle or hold grandchildren from his own daughter. Rob and I are frequently told, “how brave and strong you are”. We are not these things. We are vulnerable and fragile, and it is the strength of our community that helps keep us upright.

It is said that it takes a village to bring up a child. We have a whole world of love and support helping us, but other parents and carers don’t. As we know the service is under immense strain and even Megan herself was working in the background seeking to help others.

Here are some quotes her friends sent to us:

“The day before she died, she was still encouraging me. “You can do this”, “I’m so proud of you”, “I’m here for you whenever”.

“I wish she knew the beauty we all see in her, and still do”

“When Megan walked into a room, she lit it up”.

“She made me smile even when I didn’t feel like smiling.”

“Megan saved my life. When I was suicidal, she helped me see a better way. I thank her for my life.”

“Thank you for bringing Megan into this world! I was able to have such an amazing friend who changed my life with her happiness and love!”

I think we will leave it there. She was love and we are grateful for having her for 20 glorious years.

Megan was a shining light in so many people's lives. Now she is our brightest star and she is lighting the way for her charity.

Megan's Space has big ambitions. Not for glory but because the challenge and need is so big.

We are willing to move heaven and earth, with the help of our star, to ensure that children can quickly get the help they need, so that they can enjoy their young lives, in the way they should. And, so that other parents do not have to endure the pain and suffering that we have.

We are a small charity with a big vision.

Megan's Space asserts that.. It's time to talk and the six key strategic strands that we will be talking about are:

Advocacy
Prevention and Education
Wellbeing and Self Care
Research
Care and Support
Post Suicide Support

If you would like to understand how you can get involved, donate or obtain assistance, information is available at Megansspace.com or visit our Facebook page Megan's Space at:
https://www.facebook.com/MegansSpaceCharity/

It really is.....time to talk.

After our daughter Megan completed her suicide after 7 years of mental illness, we decided to make a difference and get people talking about all aspects of mental health and illness.

We figured there were lots of opportunities to improve her experience, as a patient and ours as her family and support network.

So we set up Megan's Space as a charity and are developing these 6 key strands of activity.

1. **Advocacy**
2. **Research**
3. **Prevention**
4. **Promoting selfcare**
5. **Support for children and their families**
6. **Post suicide support**

If you would like to join the conversation, please like and follow our page and you can visit the website to see how you can get involved.

If you would like to talk to us to see if we can help please send a private message to this page. However, if you need urgent help please approach the appropriate agency.

Help in an Emergency

Megan's Space is not able to provide any direct support or advice to individuals in mental distress. If you need support or advice urgently, there are a number of places you can get in touch with.

If you are in distress, or in need of urgent help, you can find more information on who to contact on the next page, or you can refer to

our National Signposting Directory.

If you need advocacy, then you can find all the local advocacy services in your area on the Scottish Independent Advocacy Alliance website: https://www.siaa.org.uk/find-advocate.

ChildLine:
ChildLine is a counselling service for children and young people. You can contact ChildLine anytime and in these ways; You can phone, send an email, have a 1-2-1 chat, send a message to Ask Sam and you can post messages to the ChildLine message boards. Visit the website to find out more.
Call: 0800 1111
Visit: www.childline.org.uk

Samaritans:
Samaritans provides confidential non-judgmental emotional support for anyone who is struggling to cope – you don't have to be suicidal. The service is available 24 hours a day, seven days a week.
Call: 116 123
Text: 07725 90 90 90
Visit: www.samaritans.org
Email: jo@samaritans.org

NHS 24:
NHS 24 is a call centre operated by the NHS to provide patients with health advice and help over the phone when your usual GP services aren't available. Referrals can also be made over the phone to crisis support and other mental health professionals outside normal GP practice working hours.
Call: 111 or if you think you need an emergency ambulance, call 999 and speak to the operator
Visit: www.nhs24.com

Printed in Great Britain
by Amazon

47475793R00130